Terri Wheldon

THEIR FACES TOWARD ZION

∽ Voices and Images of the Trek West ∽

THEIR FACES TOWARD ZION

Voices and Images of the Trek West

Richard Neitzel Holzapfel

Bookcraft
Salt Lake City, Utah

Bookcraft is a registered trademark of Bookcraft, Inc.

Library of Congress Catalog Card Number: 96–85532
ISBN 1–57008–266–9

First Printing, 1996

Printed in the United States of America

For my grandmother
Rachel Leona Johnson McDaniel,
born on Christmas day 1905 in a Latter-day Saint settlement in
southeastern Idaho

*G*ive Thy Holy Spirit unto my brethren, unto whom I write; send Thine angels to guard them, and deliver them from all evil; and when they turn *their faces toward Zion*, and bow down before Thee and pray, may their sins never come up before Thy face; neither have place in the book of Thy remembrance; and may they depart from all their iniquities. Provide food for them as Thou doest for the ravens; provide clothing to cover their nakedness, and houses that they may dwell therein; give unto them friends in abundance, and let their names be recorded in the Lamb's book of life, eternally before Thy face. Amen.

—Joseph Smith, 10 December 1833[1]

Contents

Israel, Israel, God is calling,
Calling thee from lands of woe.
Babylon the great is falling;
God shall all her tow'rs o'erthrow.
Come to Zion, come to Zion
Ere his floods of anger flow.
Come to Zion, come to Zion
Ere his floods of anger flow.

Israel! Israel! Canst thou linger
Still in error's gloomy ways?
Mark how judgment's pointing finger
Justifies no vain delays.
Come to Zion, come to Zion!
Zion's walls shall ring with praise.
Come to Zion, come to Zion!
Zion's walls shall ring with praise.

—Richard Smyth, immigrant
from Ireland in 1863

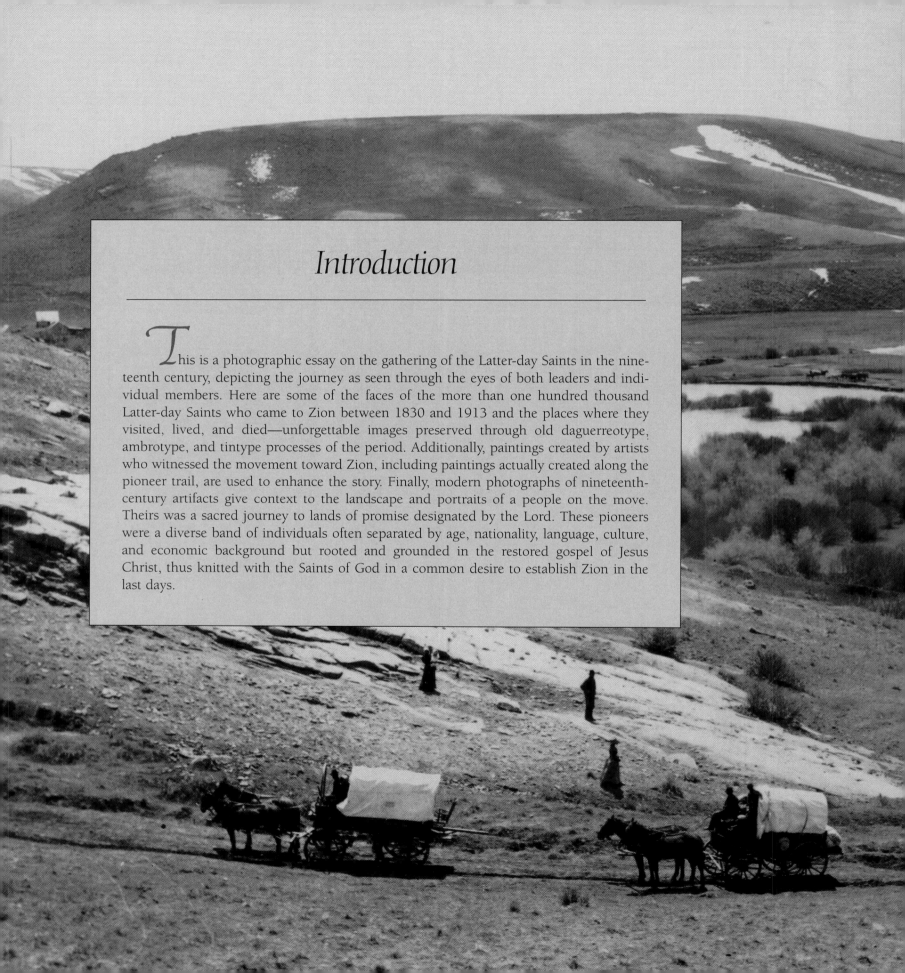

Introduction

$\mathcal{T}$his is a photographic essay on the gathering of the Latter-day Saints in the nineteenth century, depicting the journey as seen through the eyes of both leaders and individual members. Here are some of the faces of the more than one hundred thousand Latter-day Saints who came to Zion between 1830 and 1913 and the places where they visited, lived, and died—unforgettable images preserved through old daguerreotype, ambrotype, and tintype processes of the period. Additionally, paintings created by artists who witnessed the movement toward Zion, including paintings actually created along the pioneer trail, are used to enhance the story. Finally, modern photographs of nineteenth-century artifacts give context to the landscape and portraits of a people on the move. Theirs was a sacred journey to lands of promise designated by the Lord. These pioneers were a diverse band of individuals often separated by age, nationality, language, culture, and economic background but rooted and grounded in the restored gospel of Jesus Christ, thus knitted with the Saints of God in a common desire to establish Zion in the last days.

*A*lthough we generally picture the nineteenth-century Saints as those who traveled in covered wagons or pulled and pushed handcarts to Salt Lake City between 1847 and 1869, many of their diaries, letters, and reminiscences reveal quite a different story.

First, the pioneer trail did not simply begin at Winter Quarters, Nauvoo, or Liverpool. For many nineteenth-century converts these places embedded in our collective memory were just starting points for one of the many segments of an incredible journey that began in Scandinavia, Iceland, Europe, South Africa, India, the islands of the South Pacific, Upper Canada, New England, the central and southern United States, and the British Isles.

Second, the journey did not always end in Salt Lake City but often continued to one of more than seven hundred settlements throughout the North American West (and a few designated gathering places in the Pacific), founded by the Latter-day Saints.

Third, most pioneers made at least part of the journey to Zion on a ship, canal boat, riverboat, or train.

Fourth, many of those who did come by covered wagon did not ride but walked to Church headquarters or to one of the far-flung settlements.

Fifth, the artificial division between those who gathered before the coming of the railroad to Utah in 1869 and those who came later does not reveal the true nature of the pioneering and colonizing effort of the Saints well into the early twentieth century. In fact, many "Pullman pioneers" arriving in Utah by train after 1869 loaded their belongings into wagons and made a difficult and courageous journey to new settlements far away from Church headquarters, traveling farther in this last leg of their journey in covered wagons than some of the pioneers of the late 1860s.

Sixth, the way to Zion was not a one-way road. Hardly a pioneer company on their way to Church headquarters did not meet someone heading in the opposite direction on Church assignment.

Seventh, sadly some LDS emigrants fell away during the trek to Zion and began new lives without the gospel that originally brought them from their native lands. Others lost their faith once they arrived in Zion, eventually returning east, even back to Europe in some cases, or continuing west to California, vanishing from our history.

Eighth, there is a propensity to emphasize the suffering and death of the pioneers and in some cases inflate the number of those who died while making their way to Zion. (The number six thousand for the trek on the plains apparently is too large.)[1] Yes, there was hardship and death, but the incredible story is that more did not die. Of course, there were exceptions, such as the 1856 Willie and Martin handcart companies and the 1852 *Saluda* riverboat explosion (see pp. 103, 134–36), but given the fact that Latter-day Saint emigrating companies generally had high percentages of young children and aging converts and a number of sick and infirm individuals, it is amazing that so many arrived safely to their new home. Yet even with the handcart and wagon companies caught in the snows in 1856, the real drama is found not in the suffering and death but in the humanitarian and heroic efforts to save them.

Ninth, the people who traveled to Zion were real individuals with passions, expectations, and dreams who on occasion exhibited human frailties as well as the highest qualities of Christianity. They could sacrifice much for deeply held commitments—something difficult to grasp by those who do not share their values.

Finally, the pioneer story does not end once these passionate and courageous people settled in permanent homes for the last time. Getting to Zion and colonizing the vast region of the North American West was just part of their sacred journey. While they established a very real physical community, these pioneers began to establish "a kingdom of priests, and an holy nation" (Exodus 19:6) focused on temple worship and salvation for the dead. Long before the Genealogical Society of Utah was established in 1894, family history research and proxy temple work deeply rooted itself in Zion's soil, fulfilling the vision of their martyred prophet, Joseph Smith: "Let us, therefore, as a church and a people, and as Latter-day Saints, offer unto the Lord an offering in righteousness; and let us present in his holy temple, when it is finished, a book containing the records of our dead, which

Latter-day Saint emigrant camp, by M. Jules Remy, about 1852

shall be worthy of all acceptance" (D&C 128:24; see also vv. 19, 22–23). The pioneers gathered what information they could and went to the temple to stand as proxy for friends and family who had gone on before. Nineteenth-century "Temple Record" books can still be found in an attic, an old trunk, or a cabinet at Grandmother's house. They are visual reminders of the legacy of the gathering of Saints—the spiritual gathering of God's children under the new and everlasting covenant.

For most Latter-day Saints, the conviction to go to Zion had a decisive impact on their lives. A statement by a young English convert, Jane Robinson, encapsulates the feeling of most of the Saints who turned their faces toward Zion: "I believed in the principle of the gathering and felt it my duty to go although it was a severe trial to me, in my feelings to leave my native land and the pleasing associations that I had formed there; but my heart was fixed. I knew in whom I had trusted and with the fire of Israel's God burning in my bosom, I forsook home."[2]

From the call to "go to the Ohio" in December 1830 (D&C 37:1) through the early twentieth century, the Church organized companies of Saints to boldly fulfill the vision given to Joseph Smith by the Lord to establish Zion. Many of the Saints' sacrifices, joys, victories, and accomplishments are well known. The incredible drama of faithful individuals and families fulfilling the commandments of the Lord continues today as an ever increasing number of modern-day pioneers begin their sacred journey of establishing Zion throughout the world in preparation for the second coming of Jesus Christ. Their "hearts are fixed," and "with the fire of Israel's God burning" in their bosoms, they begin the journey back home to God.

The Sacred Journey Begins

*I*n the spring of 1847, 148 individuals gathered by the Platte River near Winter Quarters, Nebraska, and turned their eyes toward the West. On 19 April they hitched their dreams to their covered wagons and set out to walk over one thousand miles to a promised land in the Great Basin. Thus the most famous of all Latter-day Saint treks began. Yet this was not the first time the Saints demonstrated their faith in the promises of God, in themselves, and in the prophetic leadership of the Church by beginning a new journey to establish a modern Zion.

*T*he movement to establish the kingdom of God in the last days actually began with one family, that of Joseph and Lucy Mack Smith. Migration to the advancing American frontier was one of the dominant forces shaping their social world. Between 1803 and 1811 all of the Smith family's moves were in a tiny circle around Tunbridge, Randolph, Royalton, and Sharon, Vermont (birthplace of Joseph Smith Jr. in 1805). The circle then enlarged when they relocated twenty miles away across the Connecticut River to Lebanon, New Hampshire, in 1811. In 1814 the family returned to Vermont and moved to a rented farm in Norwich. Finally they separated themselves in 1816 from family and friends and removed to Palmyra, New York, some three hundred miles west. The movement toward Zion had begun. Their physical and social separation from New England played a fundamental role in their circumstantial preparations for the Restoration.

When the Smith family arrived in western New York, the great religious revivals of 1816 and 1817 were in progress. Beginning with the visitation of the Father and the Son in 1820 and throughout the decade, the major founding events of the Restoration—the restoration of the Church and gospel of Jesus Christ—transpired, culminating in the organization of the Church of Christ on 6 April 1830 in Fayette, New York. Several small branches of the Church were organized in the area, but within a short time the Lord commanded his Saints to "go to the Ohio" (D&C 37:1). By the first anniversary of the establishment of the restored Church, the small band of Saints were relocating from various New York sites to Kirtland, Ohio, fulfilling the revelation to gather together to build Zion.

LEFT: *The Prophet Joseph Smith, portrait attributed to Danquart Anton Weggeland, about 1875*

oseph Knight, a member of the Colesville Branch in Broome County, New York, recalls the first gathering to Ohio in 1831:

> In the fall of 1830 we had a revelation to go to the state of Ohio, the persecution was so great that my father and Joseph [Smith] started in the winter. I started on foot alone to tell some of the brethren on the road who had joined through the fall and winter. In 1831 we met at Ithaca and came to Buffalo together and stopped there on account of ice. I and a few others started on foot to prepare a place in Ohio, we travelled 40 miles, went on board a steamboat, landed at Fairport near the mouth of Grand River; we went to Kirtland, Ohio.[1]

Joseph Knight Jr., portrait by an unknown artist, about 1831

Fairport Harbor, Fairport, Ohio, about 1858

*T*he Colesville Branch was the first to respond to follow the Prophet to Ohio in April 1831. The Knight family was among the group that followed the Old State Road toward Ithaca, boarding a boat on Cayuga Lake and transferring to the Cayuga and Seneca Canal, which eventually connected with the Erie Canal. Soon two other groups—the Palmyra and Fayette Saints—made their way west, utilizing the Erie Canal. Lucy Mack Smith recalls her experience in the spring of 1831:

> When the brethren considered the spring sufficiently open for traveling on the water, we all began to prepare for our removal to Kirtland. We hired a boat of a certain Methodist preacher, and appointed a time to meet at our house, for the purpose of setting off together; and when we were thus collected, we numbered eighty souls. . . .
>
> I then called the brethren and sisters together, and reminded them that we were traveling by the commandment of the Lord, as much as Father Lehi was, when he left Jerusalem; and, if faithful, we had the same reasons to expect the blessings of God. . . . We then seated ourselves and sang a hymn. The captain was so delighted with the music, that he called to the mate, saying, "Do, come here, and steer the boat; for I must hear that singing." . . .
>
> At the approach of sunset, we seated ourselves, and sang another hymn. The music sounded beautifully upon the water, and had a salutary effect upon every heart, filling our souls with love and gratitude to God, for his manifold goodness towards us.[2]

After leaving their homes, the Saints reached Buffalo, where they boarded a Lake Erie steamer to make the 150-mile voyage to Fairport Harbor at Painesville, Ohio, only a few miles from the gathering place at Kirtland. The harbor became the hub of Latter-day Saint movement, and like most of the roads utilized by the Saints, Fairport Harbor saw converts coming and missionaries going.

LEFT: *The Erie Canal, painting by John Hill, about 1830*

By far the most important building in Kirtland was the temple, one of the major features of the Restoration, which made the gathering place a temple-city. The Saints began construction of this "House of the Lord" in 1833 and dedicated it in March 1836 with a period of great Pentecostal outpourings upon the Saints. Of course, this was not the culmination of the Lord's blessings for the Saints, as he revealed in Doctrine and Covenants 110:

> For behold, I have accepted this house, and my name shall be here; and I will manifest myself to my people in mercy in this house. . . .
> Yea the hearts of thousands and tens of thousands shall greatly rejoice in consequence of the blessings which shall be poured out, and the endowment with which my servants have been endowed in this house.
> And the fame of this house shall spread to foreign lands; and this is the beginning of the blessing which shall be poured out upon the heads of my people. (Vv. 7, 9–10.)

Kirtland Temple, about 1880

$\mathcal{I}$n the summer of 1831, the elders of the Church were commanded to go to Missouri, where the land of inheritance was to be made known. After their arrival the Lord told them: "This land, which is the land of Missouri, . . . is the land which I have appointed and consecrated for the gathering of the saints. Wherefore, this is the land of promise, and the place for the city of Zion. . . . Behold, the place which is now called Independence is the center place; and a spot for the temple is lying westward, upon a lot which is not far from the courthouse." (D&C 57:1–5.)

Eight hundred Saints gathered in Jackson County, establishing five settlements. However, they were driven from their homes, farms, and temple site. Eventually, a large settlement was established at Far West, Caldwell County, Missouri. Some went even farther north and laid out a settlement designated "Adam-ondi-Ahman." In northwest Missouri the Lord gave another revelation as recorded in Doctrine and Covenants 115, revealing the sacred nature of the land:

> Verily I say unto you all: Arise and shine forth, that thy light may be a standard for the nations;
>
> And that the gathering together upon the land of Zion, and upon her stakes, may be for a defense, and for a refuge from the storm, and from wrath when it shall be poured out without mixture upon the whole earth.
>
> Let the city, Far West, be a holy and consecrated land unto me; and it shall be called most holy, for the ground upon which thou standest is holy.
>
> Therefore, I command you to build a house unto me, for the gathering together of my saints, that they may worship me. (Vv. 5–8.)

The metaphor "stakes," which is associated with geographical areas of the Church, is from the book of Isaiah: "Enlarge the place of thy tent [temple or tabernacle], and let them stretch forth the curtains of thy habitations: spare not, lengthen thy cords, and strengthen thy stakes" (Isaiah 54:2).

Isaiah's rich imagery associates the concept of "stake" with the tent pegs that firmly held the curtains around the tabernacle that Moses built, the central Israelite sanctuary and seat of the Lord. In this sense, the great city of New Jerusalem in Jackson County will be the "tent" of the Lord, the place of his temple and his throne. Zion is the temple-city par excellence. The temple is at the heart of the New Jerusalem. "Verily this is the word of the Lord, that the city New Jerusalem shall be built by the gathering of the saints, beginning at this place, even the place of the temple" (D&C 84:4). While the Saints waited to redeem Zion, they were to gather to her stakes and establish temple-cities where the Lord designated.

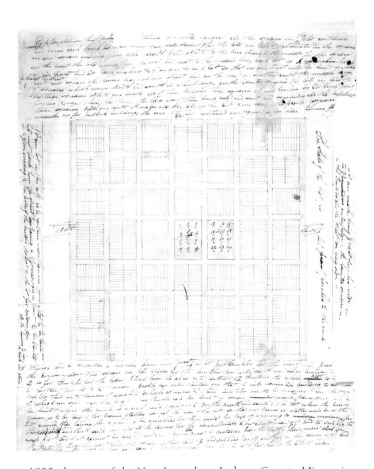

1833 plat map of the New Jerusalem, Jackson County, Missouri

LEFT: *"Leaving Missouri," painting by C.C.A. Christensen*

Brigham Young, daguerreotype by Lucian Foster, about 1844

ut even as the Saints tried to build Zion, persecution raised its head again and they were expelled from the state, forced to leave their homes, businesses, and farms, while many Church leaders were held in Missouri prisons. Several thousand members left Missouri during the winter of 1838–39 and went east to Illinois and Iowa, seeking refuge from the mobs and state militia in northern Missouri. Their escape to Illinois was accomplished as fast as eight days and as long as three weeks. Emma Smith made her departure from Far West with a group of Saints on 7 February 1839 and wrote her husband shortly thereafter:

> No one but God knows the reflections of my mind and the feelings of my heart when I left our house and home, and almost all of everything that we possessed excepting our little children, and took my journey out of the State of Missouri, leaving you shut up in that lonesome prison. But the reflection is more than human nature ought to bear, and if God does not record our sufferings and avenge our wrongs on them that are guilty, I shall be sadly mistaken.[3]

righam Young led the wintertime exodus from the promised land of Zion in Missouri to Illinois. Within a short few years after the city of Nauvoo was established, Brother Brigham stood as the Lord's prophet on the earth following the martyrdom of Joseph and his brother Hyrum on 27 June 1844. The question as to whether to abandon Nauvoo before completing the temple to avoid further conflict with the non-Latter-day Saints in the region was upon his mind in January 1845. Brigham Young recorded the following in his journal: "Friday, January 24. Brothers Heber C. Kimball and Newell K. Whitney were at my house. We washed, anointed, and prayed. Had a good time. I inquired of the Lord whether we should stay here and finish the Temple. The answer was we should."[4]

He hastened to fulfill the martyred Prophet's vision to complete the Nauvoo Temple so the Saints could receive their temple blessing before they fled into the wilderness. This drama is one of the most inspiring in the history of the Church.

Despite continued harassment by anti-Mormons, the temple was far enough along by October 1845 that with "inexpressible joy and great gratification" the Saints met within its walls for conference.[5] During the prayer of dedication Brother Brigham presented it as "thus far completed, as a monument of the saints' liberality, fidelity, and faith."[6] A few months later the Twelve prayed that they "might be permitted to continue giving the Saints their endowments until all the faithful should be clothed with the Keys and Powers of the Priesthood."[7] Spending time preparing for the exodus west did not stop President Young and a group of temple workers from spending long hours, sometimes day and night, administering the ordinances to some six thousand men and women before abandoning the City of Joseph.

Richards family, daguerreotype by Lucian Foster, 26 March 1845

*T*his copy of an original daguerreotype of the Richards family shows Jennetta Richards sitting on the lap of her husband, Willard, as their son, Heber John, cuddles close to his father. This view became an important treasure for Willard Richards, as his beloved companion, Jennetta, fell ill on 21 May and died on 9 July 1845. It represents

something more important than a family heirloom, however. On 29 May 1843, Willard Richards and Jennetta Richards were able to be "sealed" by priesthood authority, which promised them a union beyond death.[8] Willard's faith in the promises of the Lord is felt in the words recorded in his diary on the day Jennetta was buried and in the fact that he clothed her in white temple robes, possibly the first such instance in the modern dispensation:

> Friday, July 11. At dinner Rhoda Ann [nearly two years old] spoke out very pleasantly and said, "Ma is gone away. She is gone to see Uncle Joseph and Hyrum and my little brother." I wept for joy to think of the happy meeting of Jennetta and Heber John.[9] About sunset [we] laid the coffin in a pine box in a vault. . . . [I threw] a dahlia on the head of the coffin in the vault and said, "I will come and fetch it with [you]."[10]

*I*n the 31 December 1845 issue of a Boston weekly, *The Odd Fellow*, a report about the expected departure of the Saints indicates:

> One of the most interesting, and it may be, remarkable events of our day, is the proposed removal of the Mormons from their city of Nauvoo, across the continent, to the Pacific. They will go, not as ordinary emigrants, but as a distinct people. . . . [Mormonism] has grown as no other sect has in the history of the world, and, so far from dying out, as it was predicted it would, with the death of the Smiths, it has grown more vigorously. . . . Next spring will witness their flitting. The Mormons propose going in bodies as large as can find sustenance, and the broad prairies of the West will be covered with their long processions of men, women, and children, their flocks, [and] their herds.[11]

The Saints sorrowfully left their newly completed temple for the wilderness of Iowa, but rejoiced in the blessing they had received in the House of the Lord and hoped that another temple could be built once they located a new land of promise.

Into the Wilderness

*T*he Shumway family arrived at the Nauvoo ferry crossing on 4 February 1846. As they waited with an ox-drawn wagon in nearly zero-degree weather at the foot of Parley Street, they saw the temple standing above the city as a monument to a people dedicated to serving God. Soon they began their family trip across the Mississippi River, the first of many who would depart in the next days, weeks, and months.

The Saints sifted through their personal possessions, carefully selecting items for their journey into the wilderness. Three articles that many fortuitously took were journals, writing pens, and ink. Patty Bartlett Sessions began a "day book" in February 1846:

A Day Book given to me, Patty Sessions, by Sylvia Lyon this 10th day of Feb. 1846. Patty Sessions, her book. I am now fifty-one years, six days old. February 10, 1846. City of Joseph, Hancock Co. Ill. . . . My things are now packed ready for the west. Have . . . put Richards' wife to bed with a daughter. In the afternoon put Sister Harriet Young to bed with a son. 11th—made me a cap, and in the evening went to the Hall to see the scenery of the massacre of Joseph and Hyrum Smith. February 12—. . . started for the west. February 13—attended prayers in our wagon and have eaten our own breakfast. February 14—This morning it snows. Sister Oakly has set up all night because her wagon did not get across the river. I gave her and Mariann and Carlos Murray some breakfast. We are now ready to leave the bank of the river [to] go to the other camp. Three o'clock—we have arrived to the other camp on Sugar Creek. It has just [been] storming. The ground [is] covered with snow and water and is very bad underfoot. Attended prayer in Father John Smith's tent.[1]

The following day was Sunday, and Patty took time to write letters to family members still in Nauvoo and to visit other sisters in the camp. The Sessions family did not yet have a tent. On 19 February Patty notes: "It snows hard, the wind blows and no tent yet." Soon cloth arrived for the flaps, but "no twine to sew it with." On 23 February canvas arrived, and Patty began to make the tent. Two days later she trudged through the snow to "put Jackson Redding's wife to bed." A few days later, John Scott's wife had a miscarriage, and Patty helped to make the woman as comfortable as possible.

When one of the companies moved from Sugar Creek on 29 February, Patty and her husband went along. Within a few days they lost their cow, so Patty drove the wagon as her husband went to look for it. On 6 March she backtracked ten miles to help her daughter Sarah Ann, who, she notes, was "sick." Two days later, Sarah Ann had a baby boy. Patty's husband and other children were now catching up with them. By 9 March Patty and her family were sixty miles from Nauvoo: "Everyone together . . . but our cow."[2]

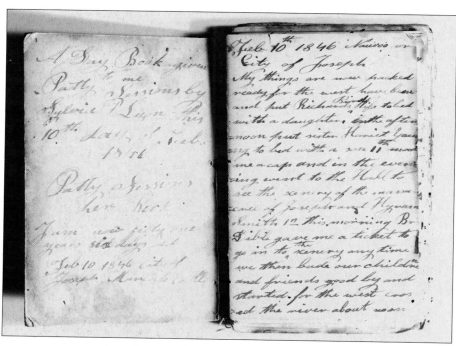

Patty Bartlett Sessions 1846–49 diary

*I*n an account of a visit to Salt Lake City, Mark Twain records his feelings about Latter-day Saint women:

> Our stay in Salt Lake City amounted to only two days and therefore we had no time to make the customary inquisition into the workings of polygamy and get up the usual statistics and deductions preparatory to calling the attention of the nation at large once more to the matter. I had the will to do it. With the gushing self-sufficiency of youth I was feverish to plunge in headlong and achieve a great reform here—until I saw the Mormon women. Then I was touched. My heart was wiser than my head. It warmed toward these poor, ungainly, and pathetically "homely" creatures, and as I turned to hide the generous moisture in my eyes, I said, "No—the man that marries one of them has done an act of Christian charity which entitles him to the kindly applause of mankind, not their harsh censure—and the man that marries sixty of them has done a deed of open-handed generosity so sublime that the nations should stand uncovered in his presence and worship in silence.[3]

Patty Bartlett Sessions, 1892

After examining Patty Sessions's photograph or one of the countless images in family albums, one may agree with Mark Twain's observation. One of the challenges in visualizing the pioneers is the fact that photography did not come to this country until September 1839. In the first few years many people were unable to take advantage of this magical discovery. As the Saints moved further west—including into the new settlements north and south of the Latter-day Saint core area along the Wasatch Front—the opportunity to have a photograph taken continued to be a difficult proposition. Even when a photographer was present, the need for food and clothing usually took precedence over photographs. As a result, we have few images from the early period, and many of the photographs we do have of these pioneers were taken later in life—long after the difficult work of emigration and colonization had taken place. Long, hard hours of toil, as well as little professional health care from either a dentist or doctor, aged the pioneers before their time. By and large, what we often see is an older person, not the young and vigorous individual who made the trek west. And in some cases what we have is a photograph of someone who was already dead. Time and money may have prevented the individual from having his or her "image fixed," but after they died, relatives often wanted their photograph. Consequently, the body was prepared and a photographer was asked to preserve the likeness of the loved one, as in the case with the Patty Sessions photograph above. She died on 14 December 1892 when almost ninety-nine years old. What did she look like when she joined the Church in 1834, nearly sixty years earlier? We picture the pioneers through the lenses of the photographs that have survived, many taken later in life. Those images stay with us when we read their stories, sometimes of events that happened decades before the photographs were taken.

uring a brief period in late February 1846, the weather became so bitterly cold that the Mississippi River froze, enabling the Saints to walk over the ice with their wagons. For the Latter-day Saints, this part of the great exodus story was the equivalent of the miracle of the children of Israel crossing the Red Sea. After these first pioneers out of Nauvoo crossed the river, they gathered on the banks of Sugar Creek, Lee County, Iowa. The next leg of the journey began officially on 1 March 1846, when groups of Saints left Sugar Creek and followed an old and established territorial road that eventually led them to less-developed roads and American Indian trails across Iowa. Certainly a period of suffering, the trek across Iowa in 1846 was long and hard—it took Brigham Young an incredible 131 days to complete the 310-mile trek from east to west. By comparison, the second leg of the journey took 111 days to cover 1,050 miles from Winter Quarters to Salt Lake.

It was during this trek across Iowa that William Clayton penned his famous hymn "All Is Well," now known as "Come, Come, Ye Saints." He writes in his journal on 15 April 1846:

> This morning Ellen Kimball came to me and wishes me much joy. She said Diantha has a son. I told her I was afraid it was not so, but she said Brother Pond had received a letter. I went over to Pond's and he read that she had a fine fat boy on the 30th . . . , but she was very sick with ague and mumps. Truly I feel to rejoice at this intelligence but feel sorry to hear of her sickness. . . . I composed a new song—"All is well." I feel to thank heavenly father for my boy and pray that he spare and preserve his life and that of his mother and so order it so that we may soon meet again.[4]

By 23 April the group of pioneers made their first permanent camp, called Garden Grove, and then established another one, which they named Mount Pisgah.

The first pioneer group left Mount Pisgah on 1 June, following another Indian trail to the Missouri River Valley and a region known as Council Bluffs. The region, a fifty-mile radius around several trading posts, was an important gathering place of native peoples. On the afternoon of 24 July 1846, Church leaders met on a hill overlooking the area. As they had done in Nauvoo, they dressed in their temple clothing and prayed. By 1 August the decision had been made that the Saints should winter in the Missouri River Valley—ten thousand of them.

Drawings of Mount Pisgah and Cutler's Park in Heber C. Kimball's diary

Come, Come, Ye Saints

Come, come, ye Saints, no toil nor labor fear;
But with joy wend your way.
Though hard to you this journey may appear,
Grace shall be as your day.
'Tis better far for us to strive
Our useless cares from us to drive;
Do this, and joy your hearts will swell—
All is well! All is well!

Why should we mourn or think our lot is hard?
'Tis not so; all is right.
Why should we think to earn a great reward
If we now shun the fight?
Gird up your loins; fresh courage take.
Our God will never us forsake;
And soon we'll have this tale to tell—
All is well! All is well!

We'll find the place which God for us prepared,
Far away in the west,
Where none shall come to hurt or make afraid;
There the Saints will be blessed.
We'll make the air with music ring,
Shout praises to our God and King;
Above the rest these words we'll tell—
All is well! All is well!

And should we die before our journey's through,
Happy day! All is well!
We then are free from toil and sorrow, too;
With the just we shall dwell!
But if our lives are spared again
To see the Saints their rest obtain,
Oh, how we'll make this chorus swell—
All is well! All is well![5]

By September 1846 a site near the Missouri River was selected for the main settlement, and by the end of the month a town of 820 lots, known as Winter Quarters, was laid. On 20 December a census reported nearly 3,500 residents in 538 log houses and 83 sod houses, 814 wagons, 145 horses, 29 mules, 388 yoke of oxen, and 463 cows.

"Winter Quarters 1846–47,"
painting by C.C.A. Christensen

*S*ome among the gathering Saints did not remain in the newly established settlements in the Missouri River Valley. On 20 July 1846 a group of Latter-day Saints began what has been called the longest infantry march in history. The Mormon Battalion was made up of nearly 550 men, 60 women, and some children. The group traveled some 180 miles down the Missouri River to Fort Leavenworth, Kansas, on the first part of their journey. They eventually picked up the Santa Fe Trail as they made their way towards San Diego.

Others were on the move at the same time. The "Mississippi Saints" left their homes in the South in April 1846 and made their way to meet Brigham Young's company near Fort Laramie, Wyoming. When they discovered that the pioneers had not started their journey, they returned to Fort Pueblo on the Arkansas River to winter. Eventually they were joined by the sick detachment of the Mormon Battalion—nearly three hundred men, women, and children. Later they traveled toward the Great Basin, meeting Brigham Young's vanguard pioneer party at Fort Laramie on 1 June 1847.

*O*n 29 January 1847, the Mormon Battalion completed their 2,030-mile march to Mission San Diego and reported to General Stephen W. Kearny at the nearby seaport settlement.

Headquarters Mormon Battalion
Mission of San Diego, January 30, 1847
ORDERS No. 1

The Lieutenant-Colonel commanding congratulates the battalion on their safe arrival on the shore of the Pacific Ocean and the conclusion of their march of over two thousand miles.

History may be searched in vain for an equal march of infantry. Half of it has been through a wilderness where nothing but savages and wild beasts are found, or deserts where, for want of water, there is no living creature. There, with almost hopeless labor we have dug deep wells, which the future traveler will enjoy. Without a guide who had traversed them, we have ventured into

"Calling Volunteers for the Mormon-Battalion," painting by C.C.A. Christensen

Levi Hancock diary with drawing of San Diego Harbor and entry for January 1847

trackless tablelands where water was not found for several marches. With crowbar and pick and axe in hand, we have worked our way over mountains, which seemed to defy aught save the wild goat, and hewed a passage through a chasm of living rock more narrow than our wagons. To bring these first wagons to the Pacific, we have preserved the strength of our mules by herding them over large tracts, which you have laboriously guarded without loss. The garrison of four presidios of Sonora concentrated within the walls of Tucson, gave us no pause. We drove them out, with their artillery, but our intercourse with the citizens was unmarked by a single act of injustice. Thus, marching half naked and half fed, and living upon wild animals, we have discovered and made a road of great value to our country.

Arrived at the first settlement of California, after a single day's rest, you cheerfully turned off from the route to this point of promised repose, to enter upon a campaign, and meet, as we supposed, the approach of an enemy; and this too, without even salt to season your sole subsistence of fresh meat.

Lieutenants A. J. Smith and George Stoneman, of the First Dragoons, have shared and given valuable aid in all these labors.

Thus, volunteers, you have exhibited some high and essential qualities of veterans. But much remains undone. Soon, you will turn your attention to the drill, to system and order, to forms also, which are all necessary to the soldier.

By order
Lieut. Colonel P. St. George Cooke
P. C. Merrill, Adjutant[6]

Eventually discharged on 16 July (eighty-one reenlisted for six more months of service), the majority of the group headed towards the Great Salt Lake Valley. Some stayed at Sutter's Fort in Northern California during the winter and witnessed the discovery of gold there in January 1848.

During the whole trip across Iowa, Brigham Young was concerned with those left behind in Nauvoo, even offering to sell the recently completed temple to help the poor get away from the city. Updates on conditions in the city continued to be relayed by messengers. In September Brigham was informed that Nauvoo had been overrun by mobs driving the remaining Saints from their homes, making several hundred men, women, and children—some too sick to travel— refugees, scattered along the banks of the Mississippi River above Montrose, Iowa. At the first Sunday services held at Winter Quarters, Brother Brigham asked the Saints to help their brothers and sisters: "Let the fire of the covenant which you made in the House of the Lord, burn in your hearts, like flames unquenchable till you, by yourselves or delegates . . . [can] rise up with his team and go straightway and bring a load of the poor from Nauvoo . . . [for] this is a day of action and not of argument."[7]

The task was urgent, as few of the refugees had enough food or shelter to protect them from the elements. A rescue party had already been dispatched from the Missouri River Valley, but Brigham

Young wanted more help—a second rescue mission. As preparation for the second group's departure was being made, the first rescue party, under the direction of   O. M. Allen, arrived at the Mississippi River on 6 October ready to help the suffering Saints. A few days later Thomas Bullock notes that a flock of quail flew into the camp: "The boys caught about 20 alive . . . every man and woman and child had quails to eat for their dinner. After dinner the flock increased in size. Captain Allen ordered the brethren not to kill; . . . not a gun was afterwards fired and the quails flew round the camp, many alighted in it; . . . this was repeated more than half a dozen times."[8]

The Saints felt that God had given them manna from heaven as a sign of his mercy towards modern Israel.

*H*elen Mar Whitney records her feelings on establishing a temporary home at Winter Quarters in 1846–47:

We congratulate ourselves considerably upon being able to live in a house again, as we have got thoroughly tired of living in a tent. This, like the majority of houses, was covered with sod and the chimneys were built of the same. Each room had one door and a window with our panes of glass, but no floor. . . . Our floors [we] managed to cover with canvas or pieces of carpeting which had outlived the storms and wear and tear while journeying from the States. We made curtains serve as partitions to divide the bedrooms, repositories, etc. from the kitchen. Most of our furniture we had made to order, such as cupboards, and bedsteads, they being attached to the house; also tables, chairs and stools, and an occasional rocking chair.[9]

In the temporary Church headquarters many Saints suffered and died. Some 367 deaths were noted at Cutler's Park and Winter Quarters between September 1846 and June 1848.

*E*liza R. Snow left Nauvoo on 13 February 1846 and made her way west with the Markham family. On 26 July they arrived at the Missouri River. Later they settled into a log home in Winter Quarters, and despite the struggles of family turmoil and personal illness, Eliza notes enjoyable times among the Saints at the Missouri:

[24 December 1846] The day delightful—Sis. Gheen sent for me—spent the evening very interestingly with sis. Chase, Sessions & Markham.

[27 December] Yest. spent at Sis. Sessions—came to Prest. Y[oung]'s in the eve.—enjoy'd this eve. the pleasure of supping on a bak'd turkey in com[pany] with B. Young, J. Young, br. Benson, f[ather] & m[other] Chase &c. &c.—after having a chill of the ague in the forenoon.

[1 January 1847] This mor. take leave of the female family & visit sis. Sessions with Louisa & Zina very pleasantly. Last eve. we had a very interesting time to close my five day visit with the girls; for whom my love seem'd to increase with every day's aquaintance. To describe the scene alluded to would be beyond my pow'r—suffice it to say the spirit of the Lord was pour'd out and we receiv'd a blessing thro' our belov'd Mother Chase & sis Clarissa, by the gift of tongues.

[2 January] Stop'd overnight with sis. Gheen, visited in the forepart of the day at H.C. Kimball's, much to my satisfaction & spent the eve. at br. Winchester's with sis. Sessions & Louisa.

[4 January] Spent this day at br. Smoot's with sis. Woodruff and Markham.

[4 February] Slept with Louisa last night having return'd with her from the party last night. The party was an interesting one. . . . Probably 100 persons were present in all & we supp'd at a table that would have done honor to a better cultivated country. The exercises open'd with singing & pray'r & after feasting & dancing, clos'd with an address by Prest. Young which succeeded one by father Kimball.

[14 March] Spent last eve. in a very interesting manner at sis. Gheen's in com[pany] with Mother Chase & Sessions. Father Kim[ball] call'd in & gave us much beautiful instruction, after which we had some glorious communications of the spirit of God both by way of prophecy & the gift of tongues and our hearts were made to rejoice & praise the name of God.

[1 June] This is truly a glorious time with the mothers & daughters in Zion altho' thrust out from the land of our forefathers & from the endearments of civiliz'd life. . . .

. . . In the afternoon visited at sis. Miller's in com[pany] of Priscinda Zina, sis. Chase, Christene &c. After supper sis. Whitney, Kimball, Sessions came in and we had a spiritual feast in very deed.

[2 June] Spent the aftn. with Lucy in Com[pany] of Zina, Louisa & Emily. E. & myself spoke in the gift of tongues—in the eve. met at Harriet's; had a good time—Sis. Young join'd me in a song of Zion.[10]

Eliza R. Snow,
daguerreotype by
Lucian Foster, about 1845

The Camp of Israel

*T*he longest leg of the journey from Nauvoo to the Great Basin began at Winter Quarters in 1847. Brigham Young led the hand-picked company of advance pioneers across present-day Nebraska, Wyoming, and Utah. The vanguard company of pioneers not only found the new Zion but prepared the way for other Latter-day Saints who would follow.

Although at least twenty Latter-day Saint pioneers of 1847 left some kind of record of the journey from Winter Quarters to the Great Basin, Thomas Bullock's diary is the official pioneer company record, titled "Journal of the Travels of the Pioneer Camp of the Saints, from Winter Quarters, in search of a location for a Stake of Zion, kept by Thomas Bullock, Clerk of the Pioneer Camp." These two pages from his camp journal show the organization of the group into fourteen subgroups. The names of each male member are listed along with the names of the three women members— Clarissa Decker Young, Ellen Sanders Kimball, and Harriet Young—and the two children, Isaac Perry Young and Lorenzo Zobieski Young. Finally Bullock notes additional items and animals accompanying the vanguard company: "1 cannon, a boat, 71 wagons, 93 horses, 66 oxen, 52 mules, 19 cows, 17 dogs."[1]

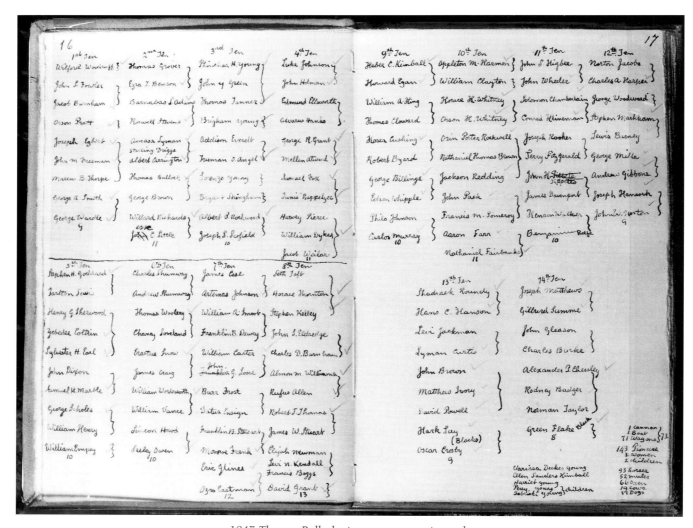

1847 Thomas Bullock pioneer company journal

efore they left, Brigham Young received "the Word and Will of the Lord concerning the Camp of Israel in their journeyings to the West" in January 1847 (D&C 136:1). This document set the organization structure for future pioneer companies. This may help explain why the Latter-day Saints were so successful in bringing so many people west. While other westering people tended to be young and healthy as they began their trek west, later Latter-day Saint companies had a higher than average number of children, older people, and the sick and infirm. Yet according to the evidence we have, it appears that their mortality rate was less than average.

Let all the people of the Church of Jesus Christ of Latter-day Saints, and those who journey with them, be organized into companies, with a covenant and promise to keep all the commandments and statutes of the Lord our God.

Let the companies be organized with captains of hundreds, captains of fifties, and captains of tens, with a president and his two counselors at their head, under the direction of the Twelve Apostles.

And this shall be our covenant—that we will walk in all the ordinances of the Lord. . . . Let each company bear an equal proportion, according to the dividend of their property, in taking the poor, the widows, the fatherless, and the families of those who have gone into the army, that the cries of the widow and the fatherless come not up into the ears of the Lord against this people.

Let each company prepare houses, and fields for raising grain, for those who are to remain behind this season; and this is the will of the Lord concerning his people.

Let every man use all his influence and property to remove this people to the place where the Lord shall locate a stake of Zion. . . .

I am he who led the children of Israel out of the land of Egypt; and my arm is stretched out in the last days, to save my people Israel. . . .

If thou art merry, praise the Lord with singing, with music, with dancing, and with a prayer of thanksgiving.

If thou art sorrowful, call on the Lord thy God with supplication, that your souls may be joyful. . . .

Now, therefore, hearken, O ye people of my church; and ye elders listen together; you have received my kingdom. . . .

. . . So no more at present. Amen and Amen. (D&C 136:2–4, 8–10, 22, 28–29, 41, 42.)

ilford Woodruff faithfully kept a diary from the time he joined the Latter-day Saints in 1833 until his death in 1898. In his diary he listed the items that certain individuals who came to Zion chose to bring with them. These possessions, kept in trunks, boxed up, or simply placed in wagons, can easily be divided into three separate categories: first, personal heirlooms and family treasures to help them remember the past; second, things they required for the journey; and finally, items they would need once they arrived at their destination. In the case of the first pioneer company, like those that followed, the wagons were loaded with items from each separate category. On 13 April 1847 Wilford mentions one particular set of items that arrived just in time for the departure of the vanguard company:

[John Taylor] brought the following instruments [from England] for our use on this pioneer Journey: two sextons, two Byrometers, two artificial Horison, one circle of Reflection, one telescope . . . all of which were exhibited to us in the evening & Boxed up so that we could take them along.[2]

Pioneer brass kettle

Pioneer bugle

Nauvoo plow

Brigham Young's compass

Pioneer pitcher

illiam Clayton makes several references to Orson Pratt's telescope:

> [Saturday, 24 April 1847] Evening I walked over to Orson Pratt's wagon, and through his telescope saw Jupiter's four moons very distinctly, never having seen them before. I went over to my wagon and looked through my glass and could see them with it, but not so distinct as with Orson's.[3]

In May, Clayton notes that a band of Indians were discovered near the pioneer camp. Later in the evening the Sioux chief and his wife came into camp to spend the night:

> The brethren fixed up a tent for them to sleep under; Porter Rockwell made them some coffee, and they were furnished with some victuals. The old chief amused himself very much by looking at the moon through a telescope for as much as twenty minutes.[4]

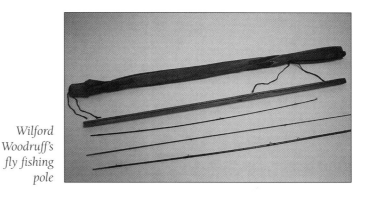

Wilford Woodruff's fly fishing pole

ear Fort Bridger, Wilford Woodruff went fishing:

> I went & flung my fly onto the [water]. And it being the first time that I ever tried the Artificial fly in America, . . . I watched it as it floated upon the water with as much intense interest as Franklin did his kite when [he] tried to draw lightning from the skies. And as Franklin received great Joy when he saw electricity . . . descend on his kite string, in like manner was I highly gratifyd when I saw the nimble trout dart my fly hook himself & run away with the line, but I soon worried him out & drew him to shore.[5]

Woodruff fished "two or three hours" during the day, catching twelve trout in all. He continues: "One half of them would weigh three fourths of a pound each, while all the rest of the camp did not catch three pounds in all, which was taken as proof that the artifical fly is by far the best to fish with."[6]

ABOVE CENTER: *Wilford Woodruff, daguerreotype by Marsena Cannon, about 1853*

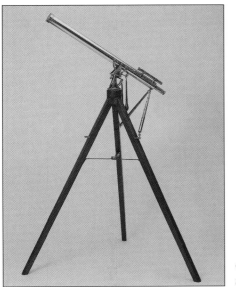

Orson Pratt's telescope

ppleton Milo Harmon left overland accounts for 1847, 1848, and 1850. The pages shown below cover late May 1847 and include sketches of some of the most famous and dramatic topographic features along the Platte River—Chimney Rock and Scotts Bluff. Shortly before this point, Harmon, along with Orson Pratt and William Clayton, devised a "roadometer" or mileage registering device to help track the daily distance traveled by the group. Previously Clayton had counted the rotations of a red rag tied to a wagon wheel.

The diaries of the participants make it clear that this was no ordinary group of emigrants. Thomas Bullock records that the Sabbath was observed "as a day of rest, for meditation, prayer & praise. All was harmony, peace, & love. . . . The brethren were called together to worship the Supreme, when Prest. Young called the Choir to sing 'This land was once a garden place' followed by H. C. Kimball making prayer to our Heavenly Father; several of the brethren then spoke their feelings, & while G. A. Smith was relating the Prophet Joseph's instructions not to kill any of the animals or birds, or anything created by Almighty God that had life, for the sake of destroying it."[7]

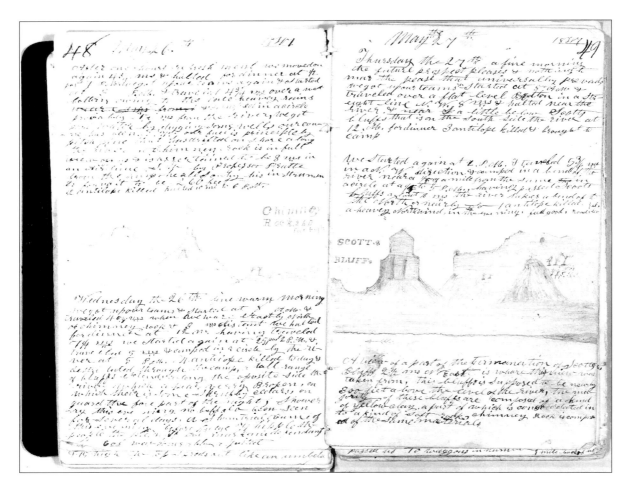

1847 Appleton Milo Harmon diary

Cache Cave in 1866, photograph by Charles W. Carter

On 12 July 1847 the company divided into three distinct groups: an advance guard, the main body, and a few wagons to accompany those sick with "mountain fever," including Brigham Young. Later in the evening William Clayton notes a visit to what became one of the most popular landmarks along this section of the trail—a cave discovered by R. Jackson Redden.

At six o'clock we formed our encampment near a very small creek and a good spring, having traveled this afternoon six and three-quarters miles and during the day sixteen and a half. There is an abundance of grass here and the country appears to grow still richer as we pro-ceed west, but very mountainous. There are many antelope on these mountains and the country is lovely enough but destitute of timber. About a quarter of a mile west from the camp is a cave in the rock about thirty feet long, fifteen feet wide and from four to six feet high. There are many martins at the entrance and on observing closely [there] can be seen myriads of small bugs. It is supposed from [the] appearance that there is some property cached in the cave.[8]

Apparently trappers had stored provision and goods in the cave. Wilford Woodruff adds: "Many of us cut our names in it."[9]

Their Faces Toward Zion

Orson Pratt and Erastus Snow, who had been sent ahead of the main pioneer company to scout a final approach to the Great Salt Lake Valley, emerged from the mouth of a narrow canyon on 21 July 1847 and became the first Latter-day Saints to set foot in their new land of promise. Upon viewing the valley for the first time, both men instinctively shouted, "Hosanna! Hosanna! Hosanna!" and threw their hats into the sky.

Incidentally, Charles Shumway and his son, Andrew, arrived on 22 July—a day after Pratt and Snow and two days before Brigham Young. One year, five months, and eighteen days had passed since Shumway and his family had stood in the chilly morning air at the foot of Parley's Street in Nauvoo with the first wagon that would cross the Mississippi River to begin the movement west.

When Brigham Young entered the valley on 24 July, the scouting party had already planted a pre-winter crop and diverted the clear waters of City Creek for irrigation purposes. President Young and other LDS church leaders were pleased with what they found. Wilford Woodruff notes in his journal that it was "a land of promise, held in reserve by the hand of God for a resting place of the Saints."[10]

LEFT: *"First View of Great Salt Lake Valley from a Mountain Pass,"* 1855

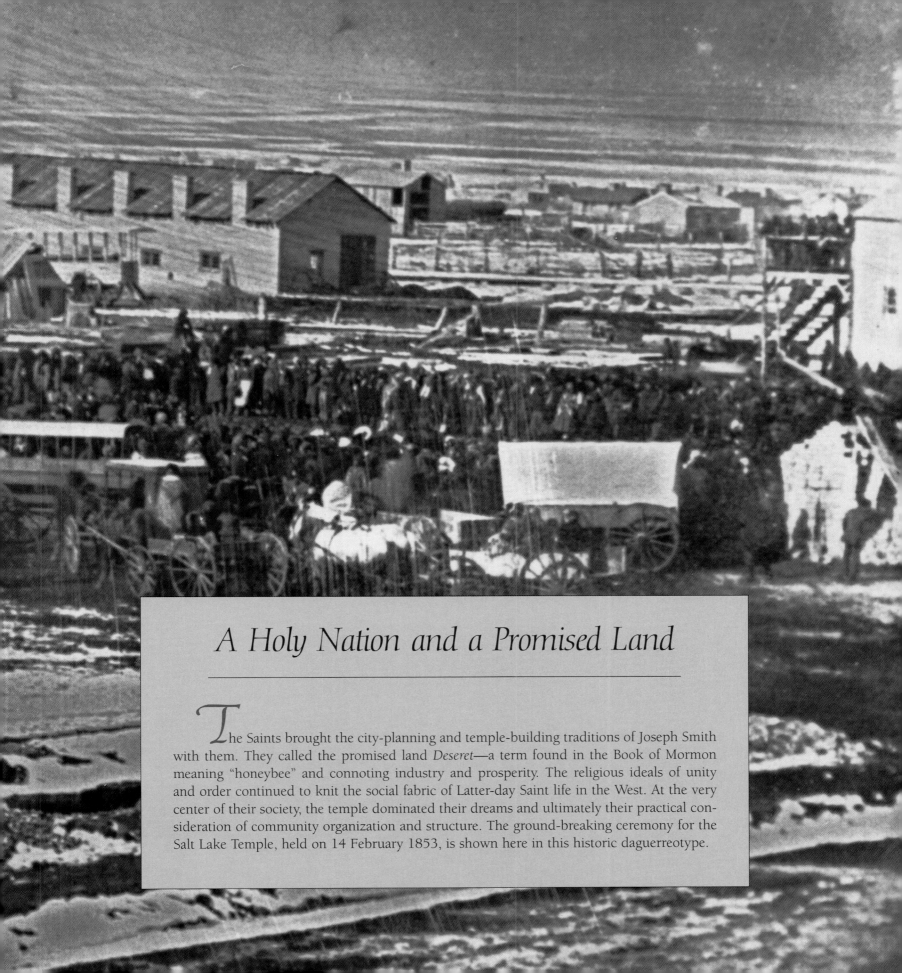

A Holy Nation and a Promised Land

The Saints brought the city-planning and temple-building traditions of Joseph Smith with them. They called the promised land *Deseret*—a term found in the Book of Mormon meaning "honeybee" and connoting industry and prosperity. The religious ideals of unity and order continued to knit the social fabric of Latter-day Saint life in the West. At the very center of their society, the temple dominated their dreams and ultimately their practical consideration of community organization and structure. The ground-breaking ceremony for the Salt Lake Temple, held on 14 February 1853, is shown here in this historic daguerreotype.

Gathering the Saints to specific geographical locations helped them concentrate their resources and energies to strengthen the Church and erect temples. Joseph Smith notes that the purpose of the gathering of Israel is "to build unto the Lord a house whereby He could reveal unto His people the ordinances of His house and the glories of His kingdom, and teach the people the way of salvation."[1] The gathering to the Great Basin would be no different—the Saints planned to erect temples in the tops of the mountains, fulfilling the prophecy in Isaiah: "And it shall come to pass in the last days, that the mountain of the Lord's house shall be established in the top of the mountains, and shall be exalted above the hills; and all nations shall flow unto it" (Isaiah 2:2).

After identifying the new gathering place in 1847, Brigham Young rushed back to the main body of the Saints in the Missouri River Valley. There he joyfully informed them that the promised refuge in the West had been found. Upon his return to Salt Lake, he was openly emotional about accomplishing the religious quest that had begun years before at a meeting with the Saints in September 1848:

> I trust I can have command over my feelings to speak with a childlike spirit yet with the confidence and courage of a man, although it may be hard to suppress my feelings. I venture to say that not another person in the congregation has the sensations that I have right now, . . . having to guard every moment to keep from bursting into tears and sitting down like a child. We are here! Thank the Almighty God of Israel! . . . From the days of Oliver Cowdery and Parley Pratt on the borders of the Lamanites [1831], Joseph Smith had longed to be here. . . . They would not let us come and at last we have accomplished it. We are in the midst of the Lamanites! We are here, thank the Almighty God. Glory to the Lord . . . for here is the place of beginning.[2]

Brigham Young, about 1850

Drawing of the Salt Lake Temple by William Ward, 1855

This architectural rendering of the Salt Lake Temple, drawn by William Ward from a design of Truman O. Angell, hung in President Brigham Young's office for over twenty years. Only four days after Brigham Young completed the trek to Salt Lake Valley, he walked to a spot between two creeks, waved his hand, and said, "Here is the forty acres for the temple" (it was later reduced to ten acres).[3] In April 1853 President Young recalled the visionary experience he had at the site:

> I scarcely ever say much about revelations, or visions, but suffice it to say, five years ago last July [1847] I was here, and saw in the Spirit the Temple not ten feet from where we have laid the Chief Corner Stone. I have not inquired what kind of a Temple we should build. Why? Because it was represented before me. I have never looked upon that ground but the vision of it was there. I see it as plainly as if it was in reality before me. Wait until it is done. I will say, however, that it will have six towers.[4]

47

The Saints named the features in their new land, giving such Biblical names as Salem to a town, Israel and Enoch to canyons, Jordan to a river, Mount Nebo and Ensign to prominent peaks, and Jacob's Ladder to a group of hilltops. There is an interesting analogue between three features in the Holy Land and three features in Utah—between the Dead Sea and the Great Salt Lake, the River Jordan (Israel) and the Jordan River (Utah), and the Sea of Galilee and Utah Lake. The similarities between the Dead Sea and the Great Salt Lake, such as the salt content and the freshwater intake of both, are obvious. The rivers connecting both saltwater lakes function in like ways. Additionally, both Galilee and Utah Lake were important fisheries, providing people with a critical exploitable resource. While many dissimilarities exist between the two regions—elevation and climate, for instance—the Mormon pioneers saw themselves reenacting the great exodus of ancient Israel from Egypt to the Promised Land. Brigham Young, their leader, became the "American Moses" who led his people to a new promised land in the Great Basin. Giving the features of the land biblical names helped create a sense of holiness for the newfound Zion.

Additionally, utilizing religiously powerful and emotionally laden symbols—such as the all-seeing eye, crowns, the handclasp of fellowship, and the phrase "Holiness to the Lord"—reminded the Saints of the covenant relationship between themselves and God, reflecting these scripture passages in Exodus and Zechariah:

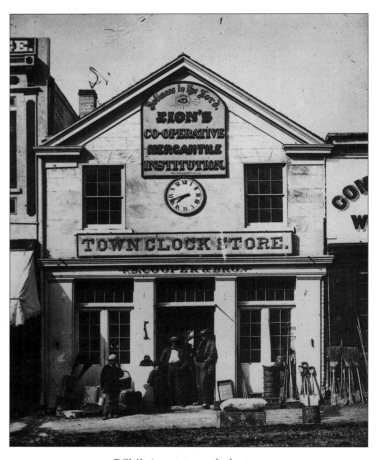

*ZCMI sign at town clock store,
photograph by Charles W. Carter, about 1869*

*1849
gold coins*

And thou shalt make a plate of pure gold, and grave upon it, like the engravings of a signet, HOLINESS TO THE LORD.

And thou shalt put it on a blue lace, that it may be upon the mitre; upon the forefront of the mitre it shall be. And it shall be upon Aaron's forehead. (Exodus 28:36–38.)

In that day shall there be upon the bells of the horses, HOLINESS UNTO THE LORD; and the pots in the Lord's house shall be like the bowls before the altar.

Yea, every pot in Jerusalem and in Judah shall be holiness unto the Lord of hosts. (Zechariah 14:20–21.)

48

*S*imilar to the sunstones on the Nauvoo Temple, the sunburst from the original Salt Lake Tabernacle may have represented the celestial kingdom or the dawning of the Restoration. As Doctrine and Covenants 45 states: "And even so I have sent mine everlasting covenant into the world, to be a light to the world, and to be a standard for my people, and for the Gentiles to seek to it, and to be a messenger before my face to prepare the way before me. . . . And when the times of the Gentiles is come in, a light shall break forth among them that sit in darkness, and it shall be the fulness of my gospel." (Vv. 9, 28.)

Those who entered the Tabernacle doorway on the south walked under the brightly painted yellow and orange wood carving, which was placed on the gable to look down on the Saints as they entered the first tabernacle on the Temple Block.

Inset: Sunburst from the Old Tabernacle, 1852   *Old Tabernacle, daguerreotype possibly by Marsena Cannon, about 1854*

$\mathcal{Z}$ion, the holy nation, was built in the pioneer settlements—the gathering places designated by Church leaders.

Movement from Salt Lake City began on 29 September 1847, when Peregrine Sessions looked north, eventually establishing Bountiful. The next year others moved farther south in the Salt Lake Valley to settle Sugarhouse, Mill Creek, and South Cottonwood; and north, establishing Centerville, Farmington, and Ogden. Fort Utah was established near Utah Lake in 1849, as was Manti in Sanpete Valley. The expansion beyond Salt Lake exploded in 1850, when six settlements were founded in Utah Valley: Alpine, American Fork, Lehi City, Payson, Pleasant Grove, and Springville. Colonization continued in 1851 with the founding of fifteen new settlements, including Brigham City, Nephi, Parowan, and Cedar City. Within a short time more than twenty thousand Latter-day Saints were located in the Salt Lake Valley, Tooele, Grantsville, Davis and Box Elder Counties, Weber and Ogden valleys, Utah Valley, Sanpete Valley, and Parowan and Harmony in southern Utah.

In the early 1850s more settlements were established in western Nevada, Southern California, and northern Idaho. Expansion continued in the 1860s as converts continued to arrive in the West. Another wave of colonization took place in the 1870s, when Latter-day Saints moved into southern and eastern Idaho, southwestern Wyoming, southern and eastern Nevada, southwestern Colorado, and northern and central Arizona. Soon communities were established beyond the borders of the United States, in Mexico (1885) and Canada (1887). Latter-day Saints went to Montana in 1889 and Oregon in 1900.

Brigham Young directed the establishment of some four hundred villages, towns, and cities in his lifetime. During the following decades more than 340 settlements were established by the Latter-day Saints, making a total of more than seven hundred in twelve western states and three foreign countries. Nevertheless, Salt Lake City remained the heart of the "holy nation."

California-bound John Grover records in his journal that Salt Lake City was "a delightful place, water running in all directions, all kinds of Business going on; took supper, the first vegetables I've eat since 2nd of May last." Because he was "worn out from the journey to this point . . . and with bad prospects ahead," Grover decided to winter in "the Valley."[5] Apparently, impressed with the community and the people, he joined the Church and remained in Utah.

Parowan settlement, painting by William J. Major, 1851

Under the direction of the First Presidency and the Twelve Apostles, members of the Church spread throughout the region. Church leaders directed exploration, founded new settlements, visited the Saints throughout the area, and in many cases lived in some of the communities at various times. Many Church members became pioneers over and over again as they settled in one area and then received a call to colonize another, as was the case with the establishment of Parowan (illustrated above).

LEFT: *Salt Lake City, photographed by Andrew J. Russell in 1869*

To Every Nation and People

*M*issionary work began even before the Book of Mormon was printed in March 1830, and by the time the first pioneers arrived in the Great Basin in 1847, it had expanded beyond the United States. Now that a new gathering site was identified, Church leaders redoubled their efforts to fulfill Christ's commission to preach the gospel throughout the world. After filling the vacancies in the Quorum of the Twelve Apostles (by calling Charles C. Rich, Lorenzo Snow, Erastus Snow, and Franklin D. Richards) occasioned by the organization of the new First Presidency, President Young called numerous missionaries to foreign lands, including many new fields of labor, at the October 1849 general conference.

*T*he important British mission commenced soon after Heber C. Kimball received an inspired blessing through Joseph Smith, who told him, as reported in the 14 April 1858 *Deseret News:* " 'Brother Heber, the Spirit of the Lord has whispered to me: "Let my servant Heber go to England and proclaim my Gospel, and open the door of salvation to that nation." ' Elder Kimball took with him one of Parley P. Pratt's Canadian converts, Joseph Fielding, and Willard Richards [and Orson Hyde]. Later, three other Canadian converts joined the missionaries and began their momentous trip to Great Britain."[1]

*S*hortly after the organization of the Church, Joseph Smith blessed Orson Hyde: "In due time thou shalt go to Jerusalem, the land of thy fathers, and be a watchman unto the house of Israel; and by thy hands shall the Most High do a great work, which shall prepare the way and greatly facilitate the gathering together of that people."[2]

Eventually, in fulfillment of the revelation and blessing, Orson Hyde arrived in Jerusalem on 21 October 1841 and soon thereafter dedicated the land for the return of the children of Abraham.

Heber C. Kimball, daguerreotype by Marsena Cannon, about 1853

Orson Hyde, daguerreotype by Marsena Cannon, about 1853

*W*ithin thirteen years after the organization of the Church in New York, Joseph Smith called four men as missionaries to the islands of the Pacific: Addison Pratt, Noah Rogers, Benjamin F. Grouard, and Knowlton F. Hanks. The elders booked passage on the *Timoleon,* a whaling ship headed for the Society Islands, and departed New Bedford, Massachusetts, in October 1843. Elder Hanks, suffering from tuberculosis, died on the journey and became the first missionary to be buried at sea. Six months after setting sail in the United States, the missionaries arrived at their first stopping place, Tubuai, in the southeast Pacific. Soon the work spread and other missionaries were called "unto the islands of the sea" (D&C 133:8).

Like other missionaries at the time, Addison Pratt left his family in Nauvoo and when he completed his mission went home to "Utah."

[28 September 1848] We found [my family] in the South Fort. . . . My oldest daughter Ellen was down on her knees, scrubbing the floor. She jumped up . . . and caught hold of my hand, with an expression that was as wild as a hawk, and exclaimed, "Why, Pa Pratt!! Have you come?" The next two, Frances and Lois, were soon on hand, and look'd equally surprised. The youngest, Ann, was out to play. She was called, and when she came in, she stood and eyed me a while with a verry suspicious look, when one of her sisters tried to force her up to me, to shake hands, saying "That is pa," when she jerked her hand away and said, "it is not," and left the room. Their mother soon came in. She looked quite natural and quite as young as when I left home, being more fleshy now, than then. At Winter Quarters she . . . suffered under severe fits of sickness, and the scurvy deprived her of her upper front teeth, and when she spoke, her voice was unnatural. Except that, I could discover no change in her. But the children had all grown entirely out of my recollection, and none of them knew me. . . . It was more like the meeting of strangers than the meeting of a family circle. I shall never forget it. In the evening our waggons arrived, and the next morning I took the youngest. . . . I opened a large chest and commenced taking out a variety of curiosities, such as she had never seen before, besides the grandest selection of curiosity sea shells. . . . And as I laid down one thing after another, I observed, "This I selected for you on the Island Tubuai, and that on the Island Tahiti" . . . and as those names were all familiar, having heard them often repeated in the many letters that I had written them in my absence, I then topped out the pile with sugar plums, raisins, cinnamon, &c, &c. She gazed with astonishment, first at the pile and then at me, as I observed, "Don't you think I was a very kind Father to remember you when so far away and make such choice selections and bring them to you?" She readily answered in the affirmative. . . . Then said I, "Step forward and give me a kiss, and these things are yours!" She readily obeyed and went about removing the deposit as if she thought herself well paid for so little trouble. . . . After a few days the other three children look'd natural and their countenances were familliar, but this one's countenance had entirely changed or I had compleetly forgotten her, and any other child of her age would have answered her place just as well, except a singularity that she has in her eyes.[3]

OVERLEAF: *Ship in harbor at Honolulu, Hawaii, about 1860*

As the missionary work spread across the earth from the new Zion, the Saints continued to teach the native people in their midst, feeling that the destiny of these people was bound up with theirs since they too were a covenant people. Even before they arrived in Utah, the Latter-day Saints hoped that the Indian

shall then drop his disguise, and stand forth in manly dignity, and exclaim to the Gentiles . . . I am a descendent of that Joseph who was sold into Egypt. You have hated *me*, and sold *me*, and thought *I* was dead. But lo! I live, and am heir to the inheritance, titles, honors, priesthood, sceptre, crown, throne, and eternal life and dignity of my fathers, who live for evermore.

He shall then be ordained, washed, anointed with holy oil, and arrayed in fine linen, even in the glorious and beautiful garments and royal robes of the high priesthood . . . and shall enter into the congregation of the Lord, even into the Holy of Holies, there to be crowned with authority and power which shall never end.[4]

In the photograph below by Charles Savage, Daniel D. McArthur baptizes a member of the Shivwit tribe in southern Utah. A. P. Hardy, standing at the right, served as interpreter for the occasion. Savage writes:

We found on arriving there that Qui-tuss and 130 of his tribe, composing part of the Shebit nation, were about to be baptized. The men and women were assembled in groups and appeared to feel as though they were about to do some important act. Their manner was as simple and childlike as could be. Bro. A. P. Hardy acted as interpreter, and when he announced that they would engage in prayer, these swarthy and fierce denizens of the mountains knelt before our Eternal Father with more earnestness of manner than some of their white brethren. I shall not forget the scene—some three or four hundred persons kneeling, Indians and Caucasians, side by side; men who had faced one another with deadly rifles, seeking each other's blood, were mingled together to perform an act of eternal brotherhood.[5]

Stereo view of a Shivwit's baptism by Charles R. Savage, March 1875

In the British Isles, the focus of much of the missionary activity centered in the mission headquarters at Liverpool. The building, located at 42 Islington Street, served as the heart of the mission from 1855 to 1904. Missionary efforts were very successful, and by 1870 thirty-eight thousand British converts had immigrated to Zion in America.

British Mission headquarters in Liverpool

*T*he first Scandinavian converts came into the Church in Illinois, Iowa, and Wisconsin in the early 1840s. The work in Scandinavia began in earnest in 1850, as Elders Peter O. Hansen, George P. Dykes, and John E. Forsgren and Apostle Erastus Snow introduced the gospel in Denmark and later to the other Scandinavian countries.

Johann Peter Johannsen, an early convert, was born in 1815 in Gudumlund, Aalborg, Denmark. He was married on 23 June 1837 to Hedvig Sophie Jensen, and the couple was baptized on 26 December 1851 by Niels Petersen. Later Johann was confirmed by Christian Christiansen in Aalborg at the Church conference held there on 4 January 1852. He records his personal feelings regarding the momentous events which recently transpired: "[I] praised my God for His great mercy for sending His servants to our country to enlighten us about the principles of the true Gospel."[6]

Within two weeks Johann was called on a short-term mission. He notes one of the common experiences of the elders at the time:

> At a report meeting held January 17, 1852, Brother Hans Nielsen was sent to do missionary work, and I was appointed to accompany him to Dokkedal. We went there on the 18th, but our arrival in the village caused the assembling of a mob and we had to leave the town, being driven out of the town by a hired man and a boy who bombarded us with sticks and other moveables, and when they couldn't find any more rocks they attacked us with clubs, and at last they hit Brother Nielsen in the head so hard that he fell helpless to the ground. I turned around to our tormentors and asked if they did not think they would be committing a sin if they killed us. They at last let us go and Brother Nielsen was able to arise and we thank God for our deliverance.[7]

Following his ordination as a teacher, Johann was sent on another mission with Niels Mickelsen in May 1852. He

"Missionaries Preaching in Denmark," painting by C.C.A. Christensen, completed in 1903

writes that in November at a conference held at Aalborg, "I was ordained an Elder and appointed President of the [Kjeldgaard] Branch. . . . I acted as President for the Kjeldgaard Branch for two years, and was then called to go on a mission to the Morso and Thyland."[8] Later the family sold their farm so they could gather with the Saints in America. The rest of the family of eight left home with 405 Scandinavian Saints under the direction of Christian A. Madsen on the ship *Franklin*. The group arrived in New York on 29 May and made their way to Florence, Nebraska, arriving on 9 June, prepared to make the final length of the trip by covered wagon with the John Murdock company to Salt Lake City. They arrived there on 27 September. Eventually the family made their way to Cache County and settled at Richmond.

The first elders sent to Wales were Henry Royle and Frederick Cook in 1840. Soon William Henshaw followed and preached in the heartland of Wales, going directly to Merthyr Tydfil. The first converts were baptized in February 1843—the family of William Davis. In December 1845 Captain Dan Jones began his labors in his native land, and during the next decade thousands joined. The final issue of the *Prophwyd y Jubili* (*Prophet of the Jubilee*), a monthly Latter-day Saint newspaper published from July 1846 to December 1848, announced: "From now on we intend to trumpet after you in *Udgorn Seion* [*Zion's Trumpet*, a new Welch newspaper], shouting each month, 'Come out of her, my people.' Mentioned frequently will be the excellencies of Zion and the law that shall come out from there, together with the best path for everyone to go to that country [America]."[9]

The masthead of the new publication contained the words from Revelation 18:4: "Come out of her, my people, that ye be not partakers of her sins, and that ye receive not of her plagues."

LDS Welch newspaper, 1861

Deuwch allan o honi hi,fy mhobl i, fel na byddoch gyd-gyfrannogion o'i phechodau hi, ac na dderbynioch o'i phlaau hi."

RHIF. 31. CYF. XIV.   AWST 3, 1861.   PRIS 1½c.

NODIADAU GAN Y LLYWYDD HEBER C. KIMBALL, DINAS Y LLYN HALLT MAWR, EBRILL 7FED, 1861.

Y mae nodiadau y brawd Snow yn dda a dysglaer iawn i gyd i bob meddwl gwybodus. Mae genym i gynnyddu yr un fath a phlentyn sy'n myned i'r ysgol ac yn dechreu gyda'i A B C. Ar ol i'r plentyn hwnw adnabod llythyrenau y iaith Saesnaeg, y mae'n medru eu gosod yn nghyd a gwneud geiriau a brawddegau o honynt. Yna y mae arno eisiau " Ail Lyfr," ac yn mhen enyd, bydd am gael Trydydd a Phedwerydd Lyfr. Gellwch chwi a minau ymwellhau yn raddol ar yr un tir, ac nid oes un ffordd i ddyn wellhau neu gynnyddu ond trwy brofiad. Nid oes un dyn yn yr Eglwys hon ag sydd wedi byw ei grefydd ac wedi rhodio yn ngoleuni gwirionedd am yr 28 mlynedd diweddaf, nad yw yn gwybod mwy gan-waith nag y gwyddai ar ddechreu ei yrfa, a thrwy brofiad y daeth y wybodaeth hono.

Dylem werthfawrogi ein bendithion a'r doniau y mae Duw wedi gynnysgaethu arnom ni, a dylai ein serchiadau fod yn gryfach tuagat Rhoddwr y doniau nag y maent tuagat y doniau. Ai fy nyledswydd i yw meddwl mwy am Iesu, Mab y Duw byw, nag am ei Dad ef, yr hwn a'i rhoddodd megys aberth dros bechodau y byd ? Pa un yw y mwyaf, Rhoddwr y ddawn neu y ddawn ? Gwn am gannoedd o enghreifftiau yn y rhai y cymerwyd y doniau hyny oddiwrth y derbyn-

*J*n the momentous October 1849 general conference, Apostle Lorenzo Snow and Sicilian native Joseph Toronto (or Taranto) received calls to Italy, which at the time was made up of several political entities united by language and strong ties with Roman Catholicism. While on his way to the mission field Elder Snow found information in a public library about a group of twenty thousand Protestants known as Waldenses, who were living in several villages in the mountain valleys of Piedmont, Italy. Elder Snow hoped to visit the group as part of his effort to bring the restored gospel to the region. He called upon two English elders, T. B. H. Stenhouse and Jabez Woodard, to accompany him and Elder Toronto. At Torre Pellice, the largest Waldensian village in Piedmont, the missionaries dedicated the land on a nearby mountain they called "Mount Brigham." Soon the missionaries visited the various Waldensian villages in the region, including St. Germain.

By the time Latter-day Saint missionaries arrived in the area the picturesque wooden bridge in the accompanying illustration was replaced by a stone one, but everything else remained basically the same, including the Waldensian Church (temple) which had stood for several hundred years. Elder Woodard recalls visiting the Henri Louis and Marie Therese Chatelain family in the small village in 1853:

I first visited them when the mother was sick and this caused the sectarians around to caution the family against the visits of a polygamist. Finding they were trying to excite prejudice in that way I went again and

preached plurality to the Father and the result was as it will ever be to an honest mind. The house soon became a stopping place for the Elders and some of the highest names in the Church have eaten and slept beneath that hospitable roof.[10]

Marie Therese, the matriarch of the family, died on 23 July, shortly after Elder Woodard's first visit. A month later Elder Woodard records another event that changed the life of the family: "I baptized several persons in the River Clusone, among whom was Sister Henriette Chatelain and most of her Father's family. . . . When the mob afterwards attacked me here Henriette came out with a lamp [to help], while the rocks were rattling upon the balcony and the ruffians were breathing out threatenings and slaughter."[11]

Henriette's father, Henri Louis, and her sisters, Marie Louise and Lydie, were also baptized on this occasion. A few months later, in November, Pierre Louis, a brother, was also baptized. Only an older sister, Marie Catherine, stood on the riverbank without entering the waters of baptism. Henriette and her brother, Pierre, emigrated on 28 November 1855 with help from the Church. Apparently both Pierre and Henriette crossed the plains with the Martin handcart company in 1856. Marie Louise and Lydie also came to Utah. The father remained in St. Germain and died there in 1862, as well as Marie Catherine, who died in 1856. Soon thereafter, most of the faithful Italian converts in the region had left the mountains of Italy for Mount Zion in the United States.

OVERLEAF: *Illustration of St. Germain Val Clusone, Italy, by W. H. Bartlett, about 1837*

Although Apostles Erastus Snow, Lorenzo Snow, and John Taylor were not assigned to Germany—at the time made up of separate city states, duchies, and kingdoms that were bound by a common language—each was eventually attracted to central Europe during their missions in the 1850s. While several individuals laid the groundwork in Germany (James Howard in 1840, Orson Hyde in 1841, and Johann Grünig in 1843), it was the efforts of George P. Dykes that gave permanence to the Latter-day Saint presence in the region. Later Elder Taylor traveled with Dykes to Hamburg in 1851, where they worked on the first German-language Book of Mormon.

In April 1849 Thomas Metcalf, private of the 98th regiment, British Army, was the first "inquirer . . . concerning Mormonism in India." His letter dated 19 April 1849 states in part:

> Dear Christian friend of the Church of Latter-Day Saints,
>   A few days ago I received a tract entitled "Divine Authority" on the question "Was Joseph Smith sent of God?" It was written, I believe, by Elder Orson Pratt, one of the Twelve Apostles. . . . It struck me with astonishment—its words were so powerful and unquestionable, agreeing with the scriptures, revealing the things that have been so long hidden. . . . I have read this tract through two or three times, and the more I read it the more I am convinced of the truth of it. . . . It came in a letter from Scotland to one of the men in our regiment. A number of men have read it and it seems to awaken all, for they wish to have some further investigation of these matters. . . . And now, dear Christian friend, I would like to hear from you, concerning what I should do to save [myself] from the wrath to come.[12]

Apparently books and tracts were sent to Private Metcalf, who received them with joy, but he died in November 1850 before being baptized.

Soon thereafter, two British seamen, George Barber and Benjamin Richie, both members of the Church, arrived in Calcutta and preached the gospel while waiting to return home. In 1851 Joseph Richards, a sail maker on the East Indian *Gloriosa,* was ordained by British Mission president George B. Wallace to be a missionary to India. Upon his arrival in Calcutta he met with members of a religious group called the Plymouth Brethren. On 22 June 1851, Elder Richards baptized four of them—the first converts in Asia in the new dispensation. The first native convert was baptized

LEFT: *First edition of the German Book of Mormon, 1852*

in October 1851, a woman by the name of Anna. By March 1852 the branch consisted of twelve Europeans and twenty Indians, including Brother "Brigham" Prankisto, who was working on translating Lorenzo Snow's *The Only Way to Be Saved* pamphlet.[13]

The Only Way to Be Saved, the most widely distributed nineteenth-century missionary tract, was written by Lorenzo Snow in November 1841 and was eventually published more than twenty times in English, as well as in Armenian, Bengali, Danish, Dutch, French, German, Greek, Italian, and Swedish before the end of the century.

যে ব্যক্তি কোন বিষয় শুনিবার পূর্ব্বে তাহার
বিচার করে সে জ্ঞানী নহে ।

পরিত্রাণের কেবল মাত্র পথ ।

অথবা

আদি ধর্ম্মপুস্তক উদ্ধার ।

অর্থাৎ

ইদানিন্তন মহাত্মাদের প্রভু যিশু খ্রীষ্টের আদি
মতের বিশেষঃ ব্যাখ্যা

আমেরিকান পাদরি এবং ইটালিএন ও সুইস্ এবং
ভারতবর্ষীয় খ্রীষ্টীয় মণ্ডলী সকলের অধ্যক্ষ
শ্রীলারেঞ্জো সাহেব কৃত ইংরাজি পুস্তক
হইতে বঙ্গভাষায় অনুবাদিত হইল ।

কোন পথ ভ্রমণকারী মুর্খ হইলেও তাহার কুপথে
যাইবার আবশ্যক নাই ।

ধর্ম্ম ঘোষক { উইলেম উইল্ও ও
জোসেপ্ রিচার্ড ।
আই. পি. মিক্—সম্পাদক
কলিকাতাস্থ মণ্ডলী ।

কলিকাতা
কলম্বিয়ান্ যন্ত্রে মুদ্রাঙ্কিত হইল ।
ইং ১৮৫২ সাল ।

The Only Way to Be Saved *by Lorenzo Snow,*
in the Bengalee language, 1852

Parley P. Pratt, daguerreotype by Marsena Cannon, about 1853

*P*arley Parker Pratt left Salt Lake City in March 1851 to go on another mission, this time to South America—another bold move towards fulfilling the commandment to preach the gospel throughout the world:

> Sept. 5—I sailed for Valparaiso, Chili, on board the bark Henry Kelsey. After a tedious and disagreeable passage of sixty-four days, arrived safe in Valparaiso, Nov. 8th, accompanied by my wife and Elder Rufus Allen, all in tolerable health.
>
> Found the country in a state of civil war, and most kinds of business at a dead stand—men's hearts failing them for fear.[14]

The work in Chile did not take root at this time, but Elder Pratt learned some important lessons before returning to the United States. Despite the lack of progress, he remained firm in his testimony of the promises of God to the people in that land.

LDS missionaries began work in Hawaii in 1850. The first group included Henry William Bigler, George Q. Cannon, John Dixon, William Farrer, James Hawkins, James Keeler, Thomas Morris, Thomas Whittle, Hiram Clark, and Hiram Blackwell. Shortly after their arrival the group made their way to a secluded spot in Nuuanu Valley, where they built an altar of stone. There Elder Hiram Clark implored the Lord to "open the way that we might be enabled to preach the Gospel on these islands, . . . have his Spirit . . . to guide us [and] . . . preserve us from the adversary and from every evil, and that the honest in heart might embrace the truth."[15]

The elders separated to several islands: the island of Hawaii, Maui, Kaui, Oahu.

Elder Cannon recounts his experience on Maui, where the work took root among the Hawaiian natives:

The question arose directly, "Shall we confine our labors to the white people?" . . . For my part I felt it to be my duty to warn all men, white and red; and no sooner did I learn the condition of the population than I made up my mind to acquire the language, preach the gospel to the natives and to the whites whenever I could obtain an opportunity, and thus fill my mission.[16]

The *haole* (white) missionaries began studying the language but found themselves giving up their rented home within a month of their arrival because of a lack of funds. However, a native Hawaiian neighbor, Nalimanui, offered them a place in her home, which the elders gladly accepted. Nalimanui's home was the site of some powerful spiritual blessings given to Elder Cannon.

Eventually, the first Hawaiian branch of the Church, the Kula Branch, was organized at the village of Kealakou on Maui in August 1851. By December 1854 there were more than four thousand members in the fifty-three branches organized in the islands of Hawaii.

ABOVE: *Nalimanui, a Hawaiian benefactor, about 1870*

*L*DS missionary activity spread throughout the Pacific, including New Zealand (1854), but it was not until the late 1870s that membership in the cities moved beyond the white population. In 1883, following the end of the wars between the Maoris and the *pakehas* (whites), LDS missionaries began their work among the native population with major success, and by 1885 there were sixteen Maori and four *pakeha* branches of the Church.

Elder Edward Cliff in New Zealand, about 1885

Ezra Taft Benson, Apostle and great-grandfather of the prophet of the same name, was called on a mission in 1855 and met with the First Presidency and other members of the Quorum of the Twelve to be set apart before departing for the British Isles. An excerpt from his blessing follows:

> Great Salt Lake City, April 13, 1856. 7 p.m. Jedediah M. Grant being mouth. Brother Ezra T. Benson, in the name of Jesus Christ and by the authority of the holy Priesthood we lay our hands upon your head to bless you, and set you apart unto your mission. We dedicate you and consecrate you unto God and unto your mission even to go to England to assist [Orson] Pratt in gathering the Saints and building up the kingdom of God, and you shall be a stay, support and blessing unto him, and unto many of the Saints; your soul shall rejoice upon your mission, for you shall be blessed by land and sea and you shall be preserved when the raging waves of the sea gather around you. . . . The spirit and power of the Priesthood, apostleship and anointing shall rest upon you and shall comfort the hearts of the poor and afflicted Saints and assist them in gathering to Zion.[17]

Ezra T. Benson, daguerreotype by Marsena Cannon, about 1853

Missionaries included not only well-seasoned Church leaders but young men full of faith and commitment, following in the footsteps of their fathers—a new generation of elders. Joseph Rich records:

> [1 May 1860] I was called upon by the Presidency of the Church of Jesus Christ of Latter-day Saints on the 6th day of April 1860 in company with about 40 more to take a mission to England to preach the Gospel of Salvation to the inhabitants of that country, and on the 1st day of May left my home in company with my Father & Brethren-in-law John Tobin. The first night out we encamped at Br. Ira Eldrege's, five miles [from] Great Salt Lake City. My Brothers Charles and John came out and stayed all night with me and returned in the morning.
>
> [2 May] There were five waggons [in] the company and thirteen . . . men, namely Amasa Lyman, C. C. Rich, F. M. Lyman, J. C. Rich, John Tobin, David Savage, John Brown, John Eldridge, Samuel White, Richard Johnson, Reuben A. McBride and William H. Dame. Left camp at eight a.m.[18]

Like many missionaries making the trek east towards the mission field, the young missionary helped pay his traveling expenses by signing up as a teamster.

Nineteen-year-old Joseph C. Rich in 1860

The missionaries in the British Isles found a fruitful harvest, beginning in 1837. Soon it was not uncommon to find several generations of a family included on the membership rolls of the Church. Samuel and Elizabeth Beddis Morgan, their daughter Martha Morgan Burris, and her husband William and their children had joined the Church by 1860. The call to Zion tugged at the heartstrings of families, as some had the opportunity to leave for the promised land before others. Elder John R. Young records events nearly fifteen years after the first generation left for Zion:

> At Michael, Dean Hill, in the Bristol conference, lived a family by the name of Burris. The family consisted of a father and mother, a son Absalom, nineteen; Emma, seven; and Kissy [Kezia], three years of age. . . . The home had been a home for our elders for twenty years. When I was there, the elders had been mobbed so much

Martha Morgan Burris, about 1875

William Burris, about 1875

> that open-air meetings had been discontinued. President Joseph F. Smith wrote me to persist in holding them; but the Saints refused to accompany me, so I went it alone. Only little Emma Burris went with me, and several times I felt that all that kept the mob from doing violence to me was the presence of that innocent little girl clinging so trustingly to me, and I loved her for it.[19]

Young Emma made her way to Zion with Elder Young, soon thereafter into the arms of her uncles Joseph and Thomas Morgan. Through their own labors and with the help of relatives in Utah, William, Martha, Absalom, and Kezia left Liverpool on 28 June 1879 on the steamship *Wyoming* with 622 Saints bound for the land of promise, joining their family in Zion.

As the gospel message spread to many corners of the world, missionary work continued uninterrupted throughout North America. Nowhere, however, did the members and missionaries experience such violence in the later half of the nineteenth century as in the Southern States Mission. In Georgia, Joseph Standing was shot to death by a mob in 1879. Five years later, a mob entered the home of James Condor in Tennessee, and during the confrontation five people were killed. Despite such opposition, more than three thousand people joined the Church. John Morgan served as the Southern States mission president. In 1882 he records the convert baptism of Georgia resident John Alexandar McDaniel:

28 July 1882—Left [Chattanooga, Tennessee] at 7 A.M. with Bro. McDaniel for the [McLemore's] Cove, arrived at Bro. Faucett's at 7 P.M. and staid all night at Mr. Bailey's.

29 July 1882—Visited Frank Rayner, John Jennings, Price Connelly, and returned to Bailey's for the night.

29 July 1882—Rode to Bro. Kilgore's this A.M. and at 11 held meeting with quite a few in attendance. In the P.M. Bro. Barber baptized John A. McDaniel; the weather rainey and roads bad.[20]

President Morgan confirmed John McDaniel a member of the Church on the same day. According to his own story, John McDaniel's baptism came about after a unique experience: "I had a very mean and vicious dog. One day two elders came to my home. As they stepped onto the porch the dog only wagged its tail—it was some-kind-a-miracle, so I joined the church."[21]

Like many of the Saints in Georgia, John McDaniel eventually immigrated to the West.

LEFT: *John Morgan on 15 July 1894*

Dutch missionaries and converts, about 1885

ohn William Frederick Volker was a full-time missionary to Holland on two occasions and translated the Book of Mormon and other important Church publications into Dutch. Returning home from one of those missions, he sits at the left on board ship with a group of Dutch Saints immigrating to Zion.

Lars Christian Johnson was born in Denmark in 1843 and baptized into the Church in 1857, immigrated to Zion in 1862, and was married in 1865. In 1881, following the death of his wife in 1880, he married Wilhelmina Elizabeth Christensen, and in 1882 he married Matilda Madsen. Both women were widows with small children. During the "Federal Raid" period, when many men and women were on the move to avoid arrest by federal officers for contracting plural marriages, Church leaders took advantage of the situation by sending many of the men on missions. Lars was sent to his native land in March 1889. Apparently he shaved his beard and went to the train depot in Richmond, passing the deputy marshals undetected. Being called on a mission was generally a great sacrifice for any family, but Lars had the additional burdens of a wife on the "underground" and another wife who was deathly ill. Before he left, Lars, a tailor by trade, made each of his children a set of clothes, as seen in the photograph of his family.

Johnson family in Richmond, Cache County, Utah, about 1889
Standing, left to right: Chris Knudsen, Charles, Sophia, Mina, Fredrick, Nora, John;
seated: Rachel, Andrew, David, Lewis, Lizze (Elizabeth—wife), Arve (baby)

Lars Christian Johnson was one of forty-eight elders arriving in the Scandinavian Mission in 1889. He was appointed to labor in the Copenhagen Conference and later in the Aalborg Conference in Denmark. According to the registers of the Heinrich Tönnies photography studio, Elder Johnson was either photographed there on three separate occasions or ordered three different photographs at different times (29 April, 3 June, and 9 July 1889). One of his letters, written in Danish, survives and is quoted in part:

Mathilda Johnson
Nykobling, 9 May 1890

Dear Wife:

I received your 2 last letters, the last written in Nampa [Idaho] 18 April. . . . I wrote you in my last letter that maybe I will be able to come home in the fall. When I was in Copenhagen I talked with [Mission President] Fjelsted concerning those matters, but if it comes to that I will go to Copenhagen the 17 September and would be home in the middle of October. It isn't sure, for I wish an honorable discharge. I am hoping for the best. . . .

Always be well is the wishes of your always affectionate husband, [Lars] Johnson[22]

Elder Johnson was on his way home in September as planned. The fourth company of Saints emigrating from the Scandinavian Mission left Copenhagen on 13 September 1890. Elders Johnson, Jens Jensen, and E. Hogan were called to preside over the company. The *Latter-day Saints' Millennial Star* re-ports their departure from Liverpool: "The ninth company of [European] emigrants of this season left Liverpool, on Saturday, Sept. 20th, in the S.S. *Wyoming.* There were 197 souls, under the presidency of Elder J. Jensen. The weather was somewhat stormy during the passage to Queenstown. We wish them a safe journey home."[23]

Shortly thereafter the *Latter-day Saints' Millennial Star* notes the arrival of the *Wyoming* on 1 October 1890 in New York City—which would prove to be the last Latter-day Saint emigrant crossing on the *Wyoming:* "By letter from Elder J. Jensen, L. C. Johnson, and E. Hogan, we learn that their company of emigrants reached New York in safety, and sailed for Norfolk on Oct. 2nd."[24]

ABOVE: *Lars Christian Johnson, missionary photograph by Heinrich Tönnies, 29 April 1889*

Thousands of converts accepting the testimony and witness of the missionaries desired to come to Zion. Many were poor and unable to make the long journey. Members in Zion, missionaries, and new converts were bound together by sacred covenants, and a way to help many of the missionaries bring their converts home was soon established. Church leaders issued the *Second General Epistle* in October 1849 to the "Saints scattered throughout the earth." Among the information shared with the Saints was an important announcement that would affect immigration to Zion in a dramatic way:

> About one month since we suggested the propriety of creating a perpetual fund for the purpose of helping the poor Saints to emigrate to this place, agreeably to our covenants in the Temple that we would "never cease our exertions, by all the means and influence within our reach, till all the Saints . . . should be located at some gathering place of the Saints." . . .
>
> We wish all to understand, that this fund is PERPETUAL, and is never to be diverted from the object of gathering the poor to Zion while there are Saints to be gathered. . . . Therefore we call upon . . . all the Saints, and all benevolent souls everywhere, to unite their gold, their silver, and their cattle, with ours in this perpetual fund, and . . . [produce] as many teams as possible, preparatory for next spring's emigration. . . .
>
> . . . Therefore, ye poor and meek of the earth, lift up your heads and rejoice in the Holy One of Israel, for your redemption draweth nigh.[25]

The Perpetual Emigrating Fund (PEF) helped more than thirty thousand individuals gather with the Saints before the federal government dissolved it as part of its crusade against the Church during the 1880s.

Across the Ocean

There is a rich tradition in LDS church history of movement upon the water, with missionaries traveling one direction and converts sailing in the other as they sought a new home in Zion. The story includes sailing ships, steamships, riverboats, and ferries. The drama of ships, steam, storms, and Saints is as interesting as any aspect of Church history, and for many early Church members who had never been on a ship, the journey to the New World across the ocean was as formidable as crossing the plains.

*T*he first ship used by the Latter-day Saints to immigrate to America was the *Britannia* in 1840. Under the direction of John Moon, the company of forty left Liverpool on 6 June 1840, arriving in New York after forty-one days. John Moon describes the voyage to his wife's cousin William Clayton, who was preparing to follow him:

[22 July 1840] I feel myself glad to find my feet upon the Land of Joseph after so long and tedious a journey; we have had a very long voyage. . . . The captain said we had a very hard voyage for the season. . . . On the 8th [June] was had a very high wind and water came over the bulwarks all that day and all was sick. I never saw such a day in all my days. Some crying, some vomiting; pots, pans, tins and boxes walking in all directions; the ship heaving, the sea roaring and so we passed that day. . . .

[10 June] . . . With regard to ship and convenience it has been bad, and I would say to all who come here, keep from Britannia if you want peace. . . .

[Once they landed in New York they attended Sunday services with the New York branch.] I told them who I was and from whence I came and w[h]ither I was going [Nauvoo]. Their hearts was filled with joy and their eyes with tears. . . . I feel glad that we have got so far on our journey. I feel somewhat sorry for all those who have to come after us. . . . You must expect great tribulation on the way to Zion.[1]

Before the year was finished, the *North American* and the *Isaac Newton* also brought Latter-day Saint emigrant companies to the United States from England. The *Isaac Newton* landed at New Orleans. During the next season several ships departed from Bristol and Liverpool, arriving in New Orleans and Quebec. By September 1841 the Church moved to economize transportation by chartering ships instead of booking passage for converts individually.

One of the longest journeys across the ocean lasted approximately one hundred days. A small group of Saints left Melbourne, Australia, under the direction of Elder J. D. Spencer on the British bark *Albert* in October 1865, eventually arriving in San Francisco on 26 January 1866.

For the most part, Latter-day Saint experiences during the transoceanic travel were typical of the period, often involving bad weather (wind, rain, ice, and heat), insects,

accidents (including falling overboard), bad food and water, insults from crew members, sickness (cholera, measles, and seasickness), being left on shore, participating in the rituals of life (birth, marriage, and death), and experiencing crowded conditions with very little room, if any, for privacy. Many travelers were expected to bring straw-filled mattresses, bedding, cooking utensils, and provision boxes. Included in the checklist was the ever-present chamber pot.

While folklore among captains and crews suggested that no ship had ever gone down with Latter-day Saint passengers, there was one such incident. The *Julia Ann* made two voyages with Saints on board, the first beginning on 22 March 1854 at Newcastle, Australia; the second beginning on 7 September 1855 at Sydney, Australia. Of the fifty-six passengers on the second voyage, twenty-eight were Latter-day Saints bound for San Francisco. After the ship struck a coral reef, the passengers were evacuated. Two mothers and three children did not make it to safety, however. One of the owners of the ship, Benjamin F. Pond, was on board at the time and demonstrated true courage and concern for the well-being of the passengers during the whole affair.

LEFT: *The Britannia*

ane Beddoe, a Welch convert and widow, and her child departed from Liverpool on the *Ellen Marie* in 1852. According to a PEF record, she borrowed $32.13 for steerage passage (the lowest fare possible) to New Orleans.[2] Additional information from the *Latter-day Saints' Millennial Star* reveals a special occasion on Valentine's Day aboard ship: "[Saturday, 14 February] Favorable winds and weather during the greater part of the week and on Saturday 14th a marriage took place on board between Edward Simon[s] and Jane Beddoe from Wales who were married by Elder Eleazer Edwards."[3]

The PEF record lists Edward Simons's account below Jane Beddoe's. He was charged $17.58 for passage on the same ship. Additionally, $8.97 was added to the account for passage from New Orleans to St. Louis, which included fare for his wife and her child. Another $7.74 for passage up the Missouri River was added to the account. Finally, $59.00 for the cost of the trip to Salt Lake City with the Abraham O. Smoot company was included. The next line "brought from above" represents the account of Jane Beddoe in the entry above. Since they were married on board ship, Edward Simons took responsibility for her PEF debt.

The family finally arrived in Zion on 3 September 1852. Andrew Jensen, com-piler of the British Mission history, notes that the A. O. Smoot group was the "first British Company of PEF emigrants across plains consisting of those who had crossed the Atlantic in both the 'Kennebec' and 'Ellen Maria.'"[4]

1852 Perpetual Emigrating Fund Company record

Joseph and Ann Harvey Day and their family departed from England in February 1853 with 419 Latter-day Saints on the ship *International*, bound for New Orleans. The voyage is considered one of the most notable in the history of LDS emigration. During the crossing there were seven deaths, seven births, five marriages, and forty-eight baptisms.

John Lyon, a member of the company presidency, records:

February 21, 1853. . . . Slept on board. 22. A Female child born [Joseph and Ann Harvey Day's infant, Jane Day]. . . . [March] 4. . . . Porpoises were seen. . . . 6. Fine weather: this day there were three meetings, the sacrament administered in the afternoon on deck. Captain, mates, and crew were present, all seemed to go on first-rate. . . . 12. Remarkable dream of Capt. Brown that

Mary Ann Day [Fluiett], daughter of Joseph and Ann Harvey Day, about 1870; by Charles R. Savage

himself, mates, and crew were all baptized in the Mormon faith, and when he awoke he found himself at prayer. . . . 17. Testimony meeting in the evening, tongues and interpretation expressive of our blessing from God. . . . April 1. Three baptized, amongst whom was the carpenter of the ship. . . . 2. A testimony meeting in the evening, much of the spirit of God made manifest by tongues and interpretations; a ship passed in the distance; a whale seen. . . . 4. Captain's cook baptized.[5]

On 6 April the emigrants gathered to celebrate the anniversary of the founding of the Church. The celebration began with the firing of six musket rounds followed by talks, scripture readings, singing, partaking of the sacrament, dancing, and four marriages. The company presidency wore sashes with white rosettes on their chests. Twelve young women and twelve young men, also wearing sashes, seated themselves with the presidency.

Lyon continues his journal entries:

[April] 13. Ship rolled much overnight; calm by 11 o'clock; a ship seen in the horizon; some flying fish seen; no land as yet seen; still on the look-out for it. Six o'clock p.m. Land in sight; great rejoicing. . . . First mate baptized; dancing on the main deck and singing on the forecastle. . . . A child of Joseph and Ann Day (from Bethnal Green) died [at nearly two years of age]. . . . 15. A shark seen; Cuba lighthouse glimmered in the distance about 11 o'clock p.m. . . . 17. Excessive heat, 110 degrees; crossing the gulf stream. . . . 20. Half past 4 a.m. Captain David Brown baptized. . . . During the day a dolphin caught; in the evening the Captain and two others were confirmed, after which the Captain and ship's carpenter were ordained to the office of an Elder. . . . 23. Arrived in New Orleans Port at 5 p.m. Doctor came on board to examine us.[6]

Soon the passengers on the *International* were transferred to two Mississippi riverboats that took them to Keokuk, the outfitting station for the trek across the plains.

British Mission president George Q. Cannon gave directions and counsel in letters addressed to Latter-day Saint emigrants who had just boarded the S. S. *Kimball* bound for the United States. Additional letters of instruction, in English and Danish, were addressed to H. P. Lund, a returning missionary whom President Cannon appointed as president of the emigrating company. Such thorough organization often drew praise.

Charles Dickens visited a group of Saints in 1863 and records his impressions of the group on board the *Amazon*:

My Emigrant Ship lies broadside onto the wharf. Two great gangways made of spars and planks connect her with the wharf; and up and down these gangways, perpetually crowding to and fro and in and out, like ants, are the Emigrants who are going to sail in my Emigrant Ship. Some with cabbages, some with loaves of bread, some with cheese and butter, some with milk and beer, some with boxes, beds, and bundles, some with babies—nearly all with children—nearly all with brand-new tin cans for their daily allowance of water. . . . To and fro, up and down, aboard and ashore, swarming here and there and everywhere, my Emigrants. . . . Now, I have seen emigrant ships before this day in June. And these people are so strikingly different from all other people in like circumstances whom I have ever seen, that I wonder aloud, "What would a stranger suppose these emigrants to be!" The vigilant bright face of the weather-browned captain of the Amazon is at my shoulder, and he says, "What indeed! The most of these came aboard yesterday evening. They came from various parts of England in small parties that had never seen one another before. Yet they had not been a couple of hours on board, when they established their own police, made their own regulations, and set their own watches at all the hatchways. Before nine o'clock, the ship was as orderly and quiet as a man-of-war."[7]

The group consisted of nearly nine hundred Latter-day Saints, including William Fowler (author of "We Thank Thee, O God, for a Prophet"), George Sutherland (later a U.S. senator and U.S. Supreme Court justice), Elijah Larkin (English police detective and later aide to Brigham Young), Lavina Triplett Careless (one of Utah's leading vocalists), and the entire membership of the Cardiff, Wales, brass band. One child died on the voyage and one was born—appropriately named Amazon Seaborn Harris.

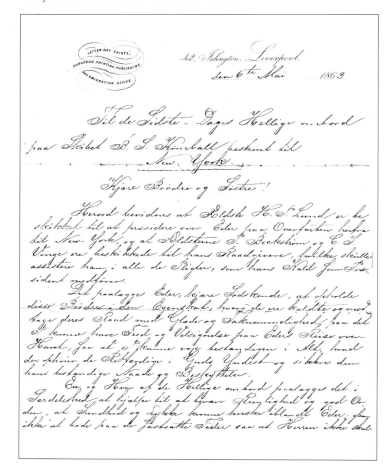

George Q. Cannon letter, 6 May 1863 (Danish)

RIGHT: *George Q. Cannon letter, 6 May 1863 (English)*

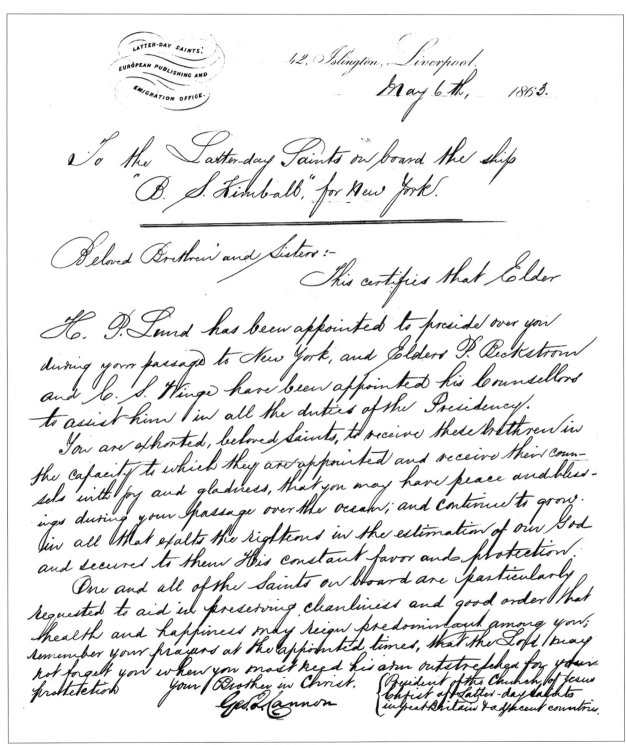

42, Islington, Liverpool.
May 6th, 1863.

To the Latter-day Saints on board the ship
"B. S. Kimball," for New York.

Beloved Brethren and Sisters:—

This certifies that Elder H. P. Lund has been appointed to preside over you during your passage to New York, and Elders P. Beckstrom and C. S. Winge have been appointed his Counsellors to assist him in all the duties of the Presidency.

You are exhorted, beloved Saints, to receive these brethren in the capacity to which they are appointed and receive their counsels with joy and gladness, that you may have peace and blessings during your passage over the ocean; and continue to grow in all that exalts the righteous in the estimation of our God and secures to them His constant favor and protection.

One and all of the Saints on board are particularly requested to aid in preserving cleanliness and good order that health and happiness may reign predominant among you; remember your prayers at the appointed times, that the Lord may not forget you when you most need his arm outstretched for your protection

Your Brother in Christ,
Geo. Q. Cannon

President of the Church of Jesus Christ of Latter-day Saints in Great Britain & adjacent countries.

Copenhagen, Denmark, customhouse, about 1890

While Liverpool was an important port of departure for the Latter-day Saints in Europe, many began their journey to Zion from other ports such as Copenhagen, Denmark; Christiania (now known as Oslo), Norway; Altona, Keil, Lubeck, Gluckstadt, and Hamburg, Germany; Hull and Grimsby, England; Leith and Glasgow, Scotland; Sydney and Melbourne, Australia; Calcutta, India; Auckland, New Zealand; Port Elizabeth and Capetown, South Africa; and Tahiti.

For many living in Ireland or continental Europe, their voyage to England by ship was their first time at sea. Except for the travelers' first experience with seasickness, the trip usually was uneventful. One company of Danish Saints, however, encountered problems with their ship and with the weather. Consequently, it took them more than thirty-five days to make the usual five-day trip to Hull, England, which caused them to miss the ship that had been chartered for them in Liverpool.

iels and Karen Marie Hansen were engaged when they made plans to come to Zion from Denmark. They received $63.00 from the Perpetual Emigrating Fund to help pay their way to Utah. Karen Marie's daughter writes: "It was June of 1868 when [Mother's] parents [Mads and Ane Marie Hansen] had given their consent for her to go to America. . . . The Saints who were leaving for America left Copenhagen by the steamer [*Hansa*] on June 13, 1868. They crossed the North Sea arriving in Hull, England."[8]

Built in 1861 at Greenock, Scotland, the *Hansa* was a German steamship that ran between German, Danish, and English ports. It transported 630 Latter-day Saints from Copenhagen to Hull in June 1868.

Hansa and Germania steamships

Hans Jorgenson, a member of the Danish emigrating company, reports:

The 13th of June 1868. Pres. C. Widerborg came up to the Hotel Aflens Yerven, and Emigrants called to order. 5 o'clock in the afternoon we all went on board the Steamer [*Hansa*]. . . . After the Saints from Malmo, Sweden . . . had come on board we started for England [at] 7 1/2 o'clock in the evening in beautiful weather. . . . We had a good passage across the North Sea, but I was nevertheless very sea sick. On the 16th, 2 1/2 o' clock in the afternoon, we landed in Hull, England, and started off by rail same afternoon and arrived in Liverpool 1 1/2 on the night. Next day we were all quartered at Hotel Columbia, owned by David Full, a Jew. On the 19th we were all sent on board the packet ship "Emerald Isle." . . . On the 20th of June 1868 we started on our long and weary journey to America, being pulled out by a tug steamer [the] same evening.[9]

The Niels and Karen Marie Hansen family narrative continues: "Elder Hals told the Saints [on board the *Emerald Isle*] that if there were any engaged couples on the boat he advised that they get married as there would be many more hardships. So mother and father were married on June 20, 1868. . . . Before the ship arrived in New York, mother's leg had become so swollen that it caused her to run a high fever. On August 11, 1868, the boat came into New York Harbor."[10]

During the three-day wait in New York harbor, thirty-eight passengers, including Karen Marie, had to be taken ashore for medical treatment. Niels Hansen remained with his wife. On 14 August the rest of the emigrants landed at Castle Garden in New York and made their way by rail towards the staging ground, when they would commence their journey across the plains.

Karen Marie stayed in the hospital in New York for two weeks without being able to communicate. Eventually "a nurse brought her clothing to her. [She] looked at the clothes and tried to tell the nurse that they were not hers. They were old and ragged and she had clean and new garments when she entered the hospital. The nurse shook her head and said she could not understand [her]. Evidently someone had stolen her good clothing and had left the old ragged clothing in the place of the new ones."[11]

Hans Jorgenson is probably making reference to Karen Marie's return to the group further along the rail route when he states: "On the 31st [August] several persons arrived from New York, having been delayed in the hospital, where they had been treated in a harsh manner. We commenced the journey on the 31st."[12]

LEFT: *Niels and Karen Marie Hansen, about 1868*

OVERLEAF: *New York City lithograph by Currier & Ives, about 1876 (Castle Garden is the circular structure located in the lower left-hand corner between the Hudson and East Rivers).*

*P*rocessing of immigrants was accomplished at Castle Garden, a receiving station on the lower tip of Manhattan Island. A former theater, it was a large circular building decorated on the inside with paintings, and it could accommodate more than eight thousand persons. Prepared to help newcomers, sometimes it was the site of swindlers and confidence men who planned to victimize the immigrants, especially those whose knowledge of English was limited. The Church stationed agents at all ports of embarkation and debarkation, including New York City, in an effort not only to expedite transfers but to protect the flock against dishonest individuals posing as agents for rail, coach, and steamboat companies.

LEFT: *Castle Garden, New York, about 1880*

Liverpool's docks were full of activity during this period. They were an important hub for the Latter-day Saint emigration. With few exceptions, emigrating Saints from the British Isles traveled to this port by rail and coastal steamers. Of the three hundred emigrant ships departing from European ports from 1840 through 1890, more than two hundred left Liverpool.

Dan Jones describes the departure of the Welch Saints aboard the *Buena Vista* in 1849: "On Monday, the 26th of February, about two o'clock in the afternoon, we set sail from the port, and all the Saints, accompanied by the harp, sang 'The Saints' Farewell' as we left the dock. Their sweet voices resounded throughout the city, attracting the attention of and causing amazement to thousands of spectators who followed us along the shore as if charmed."[13]

William Phillips and others who had come to bid farewell to the first departing group of Welch Saints threw oranges to the outstretched hands of the passengers as the ship was being towed from the Waterloo dock. As the ship moved farther into the river, handkerchiefs were then used to wave a fond farewell.

RIGHT: *View of Liverpool from the southwest, 1847*

Jane Rio Griffiths Baker [Pearce]

Scottish convert and widow Jane Rio Griffiths Baker boarded a ship at Liverpool in 1851 to begin a journey to Zion with her children.

[4 January 1851] I this day took leave of every Acquaintance I could collect together, in all human probability, never to see them again on Earth; I am now with my children about to leave my Native land, in order to gather with the Church of Christ, in the Valley of the Great Salt Lake, in North America.

[13 January] Provisions served out for a week, laughed heartily at our supply of Oatmeal. 70 pounds.

[23 January] Shift of wind in our favor, at 10 A.M. the tug hauled us out of the river into the Irish Seas, at 6 P.M. the wind turned dead against us, more than half of the passengers sick, and us who have hitherto escaped are obliged to hold on to anything that comes in our way, in order to keep our feet.

[2 February] Cooked our last piece of fresh meat to-day.

[14 February] I can hardly describe the beauty of this night, the Moon nearly at full with a deep blue Sky studded with stars, the reflection of which makes the sea appear like an immense sheet of diamonds, and here are we walking the deck at 9 o'clock in the evening without bonnet or shawl.

[22 February] At 1/2 past 5 P.M. my dear little Josiah breathed his last. He had sunk rapidly since Tuesday, when he partially lost his speech.

[23 February] Sunday—A beautiful morning, the body of my dear Boy is removed to a snug little cabin . . . where the male adults of my family have watched it all night. The second mate, with the assistance of Uncle Bateman, have just sewn up the body of our dear little fellow, ready for burial. At 11 o'clock the tolling of the ship bell informed us that the time had come that the mortal part of my dear Child was to be committed to the deep.

[10 March] I came on deck this morning before five o'clock to enjoy the cool breeze and see the sun rise; the heat is intense during the day.

[14 March] I was on deck this morning to see the sun rise; there was not an atom of cloud to be seen in any direction. I have often read of the beauty of Italian skies but I am sure they cannot exceed in splendour that which at this moment arches over the gulf of [Mexico].

[16 March] Saw a Water-spout at 11 A.M. At seven in the evening a Violent Squall came on, driving most of the passengers below, myself with a few others remained on deck, bidding defiance to the rain, for the sake of enjoying the night of the lightning, which was very beautiful, seeming to illuminate one half of the horizon at once.

[20 March] Our ship is at anchor at New Orleans. . . . To describe the scenery on each [bank] of this mighty stream needs a better pen than mine; no description that I ever read has done it any thing like justice. Sugar and cotton plantations abound. . . . Groves of Orange trees are very numerous, the perfume from which is very delightful, as the breeze wafts it towards us; thousands of peach and plum trees are here growing wild and are not in full blossom.[14]

$\mathcal{D}$anish Church leader and missionary Jens Christian Anderson Weibye was anxious to bring his family to Zion. Finally he received word to accompany a group of emigrants from his native land in 1862. He notes his preparations as the time drew near for departure: "[20 March] My wife's mother was here today and said goodbye to us. She wished that we might live well, and she cried a lot, for she still has not faith in Mormonism. We consoled her the best we could."[15]

Five days later he received word from Elder C. A. Madsen: "You must be ready to go to Copenhagen and likewise the emigrants to go to Keil from Aalborg on a boat."[16] Elder Weibye sent a message to all those assigned to leave Denmark, including Johann Peter Johannsen, a local missionary and president of the Kjeldgaard Branch. He and his wife, Hedvig Sophie Jensen Johannsen, met at Aalborg on 6 April at 6:00 A.M and set sail on the steamer *Abion* at 4:00 P.M. headed for Keil, Germany. Eventually the group boarded the full-rigged *Franklin*. As was typical for the period, a returning missionary, Christian A. Madsen, was place in charge of the group with Danish elders Jens C. A. Weibye and Lauritz Larsen as his counselors. Elder Weibye was also given the responsibility to exchange money. Sister Marie Kjøbye was set apart as a nurse for the journey. John Christian Jensen was assigned to wake up the Saints at 5:00 A.M. with music from his clarinet, followed by one or two numbers on the accordion. Anthon Lund was assigned to teach several English language classes on board. The Saints found only 160 bunks below deck, which had to be shared by three persons per bunk. The American cooks served "sweet soup" on Sunday, pea soup on Monday, rice on Tuesday and Wednesday, barley mush on Friday, and herring and potatoes on Saturday. Elder Weibye records:

[27 May 1862] Some of the emigrants carried the measles with them from home and the disease soon spread to all parts of the ship. . . . Many of the emigrants were also suffering with diarrhea, which caused much weakness of body. We lost the appetite for sea biscuits but learned to soak them in water or tea for eight to ten hours, which softened them so that they became more palatable. . . . Most every day we amused ourselves a short time by dancing on deck to music played by some of our brethren or members of the crew. We could thus have had an enjoyable time, had it not been for the sorrow occasioned by the many sick and dying amongst us on account of the measles. Up to this date three adults and 43 children have died, nearly all from measles.

On 29 May, upon their arrival in New York harbor, the company received some fresh food supplies, including milk, bread, and cheese, "which all tasted very well."[17] Elder Weibye's diary continues as shown in the illustration:

[Friday, 30 May 1862] This night slept without bedding, causing some to catch cold. In the evening at the council meeting 16 men were chosen as watchmen for the railroad cars, and C. Andersen as captain for them.

Saturday, May 31, 1862. At 4 A.M. Sister Borregaard gave birth to one girl (name Franke Emilie), and at 7:00 she could sit up in bed, and at 1 P.M. she could walk up the stairs and onto the transport boat, for we were to land at Castle Garden. At 10:30 A.M. the steamship Great Eastern came and sailed past us. At 1:00 P.M. a messenger came for us from Castle Garden, and President John Van Cott and Brother Horspool accompanied him, which made us very happy.

A drawing in Elder Weibye's journal shows the *Great Eastern* steamship. The second drawing shows an upside-down American flag; Weibye has stripes labeled red, white, and so on, with a notation under the flag reading: "Blue with yellow stars and red and [white] stripes were on Franklin's Flag." The third drawing shows the "Memorable Ship Franklin [189.5 feet] long, which carried us over this great water [3,276 miles] in 51 days."[18]

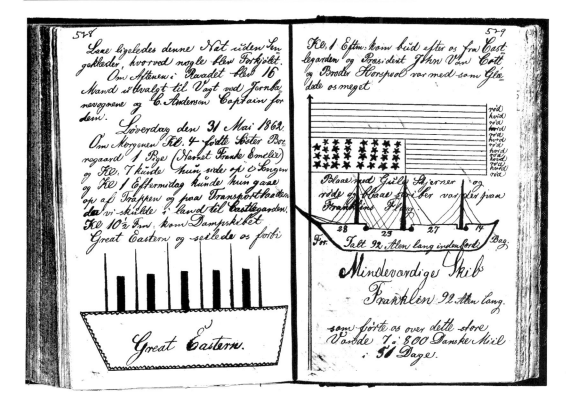

Jens Christian Anderson Weibye
diary, 1862

Between the decks of a sailing packet ship,
Latter-day Saint emigrants ate, slept, held
meetings, and languished—sometimes hatched
down in semidarkness and misery as the ship
pitched and rolled through storms.

Many of the old trunks that survived the battering of steerage ocean voyages and that crossed the continent in ox-team wagons or steam trains contained priceless family treasures. Some were heirlooms and some were parting gifts from relatives and friends whose faces were never seen again.

The china, pewter, and copper ware may have looked strangely out of place in the primitive log homes that they were brought to Zion to adorn. Other treasures carefully taken on the trek were paintings, photographs, books, and personal papers. Passed along by parents who cherished them to children and grandchildren who did not know the faces in the photographs or paintings, they sometimes just sat in an old trunk waiting to be discovered. Some items are preserved in the Museum of Church History and Art in Salt Lake City; other pioneer treasures can be found in museums run by the Daughters of Utah Pioneers and in relic halls, and still many more items can be found in the basements and attics of homes throughout the Latter-day Saint colonizing region. The treasures in these trunks, as well as the trunks themselves, are part of the visual story of those who turned their faces toward Zion.

Trunk owned by 1880 Norwegian emigrant John Rudolf Nielson. John Rudolf Nielson, who came to Utah with his fiancée, Jensine, brought his carpenter tools in this trunk to help build Zion. The inscription on the trunk reads: "JR Nilsen Saltlak Citty Utta. Teritori. U.S. Amerika."

nother important port for Latter-day Saint immigration was Philadelphia, where Dominico Bodrero landed in 1855. He was born in Lagnasco in the province of Cuneo, Italy, in 1826 on the Sabbath (*Dominico*), hence his name. Sometime after the death of his mother in 1848, young Dominico moved to Port of Marseille, France, where he learned French and changed the spelling of his name to Dominique Boudrero. One day he and some friends, armed with some spoiled vegetables, headed to a Latter-day Saint street meeting. They came to have some fun with the preachers from America, but as Dominique listened to the missionaries he quickly forgot his purpose and dropped the objects in his hands. Later he was baptized and apparently returned to Italy, as his name appears on the Angrogna Branch records of the Italian Mission.

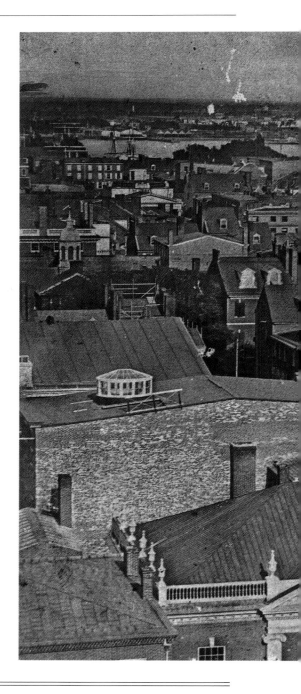

LEFT: *Boudrero family, about 1869*
Standing: Marie Harriet; seated, left to right: Josephine, Dominique (holding Harriet Louise), Henriette Chatelain (holding Lehigh)

Philadelphia, about 1840, photograph by Frederick Langenheim

With the assistance of the Perpetual Emigrating Fund Company, Dominique Boudrero made his way from Piedmont to Liverpool. He departed from England with 573 British, Swiss, and Italian Saints on the ship *Juventa* for Philadelphia on Saturday, 31 March 1855. It was a remarkable journey, with no deaths, one birth of a child (named Juventa), and no major illnesses other than seasickness and a few cases of measles among the children. Little did Dominique Boudrero know that his future grandson would marry the great-granddaughter of fellow English passengers Richard and Martha Brazier Hodges.[19] Like so many other Saints, paths continued to cross among them and their posterity who turned their faces toward Zion.

On 4 May the *Juventa* cast anchor off Cape May in New Jersey, and the next day it was tugged up the Delaware River to Philadelphia. The group continued by rail to Pittsburgh, and then many proceeded down the Ohio and Mississippi Rivers on the steamboat *Equinox* to St. Louis and followed the Missouri River to Atchison, Kansas. Dominique crossed the plains from Atchison with the company of Captain Charles A. Harper, arriving in Zion on 29 October 1855. Later he met and married fellow Italian convert Henriette Chatelain in Provo, and they made their home in Cache Valley.

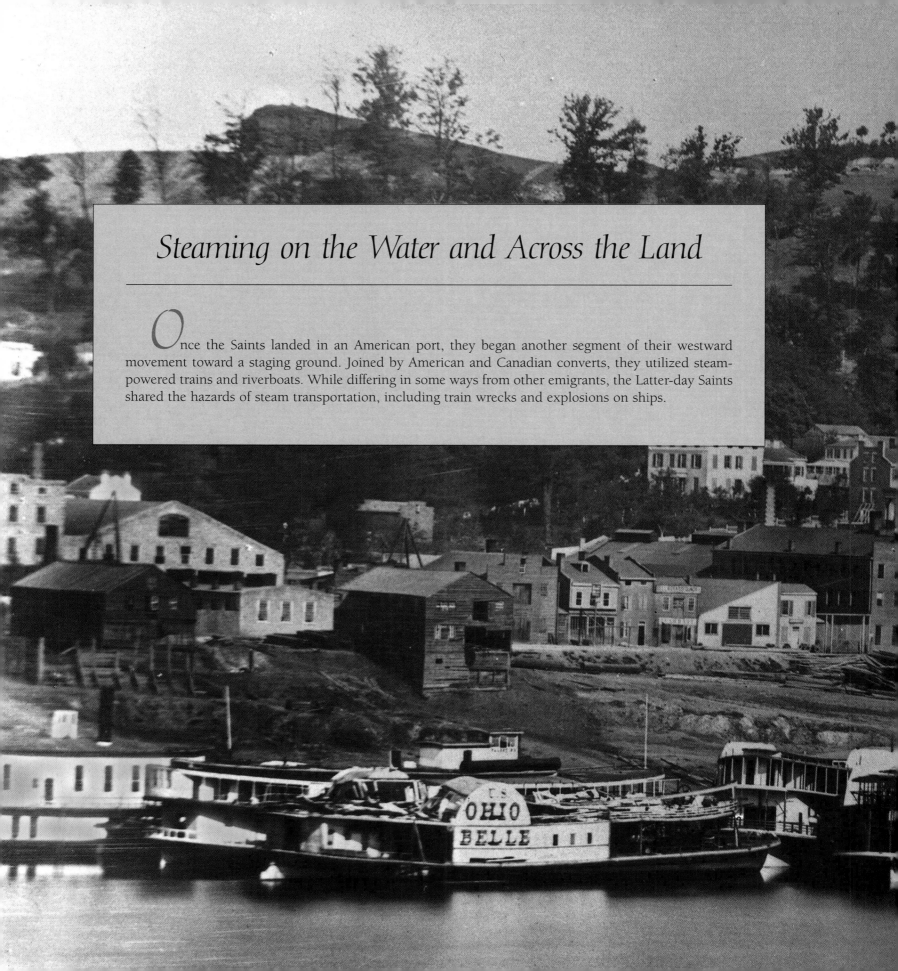

Steaming on the Water and Across the Land

Once the Saints landed in an American port, they began another segment of their westward movement toward a staging ground. Joined by American and Canadian converts, they utilized steam-powered trains and riverboats. While differing in some ways from other emigrants, the Latter-day Saints shared the hazards of steam transportation, including train wrecks and explosions on ships.

*N*ew Orleans was the major port of arrival for Latter-day Saint immigrant ships between 1840 and 1855. A few early groups arrived in New York and Quebec. Beginning in 1855, most of the ships arrived in New York, Philadelphia, or Boston. A few others arrived in San Diego and San Francisco.

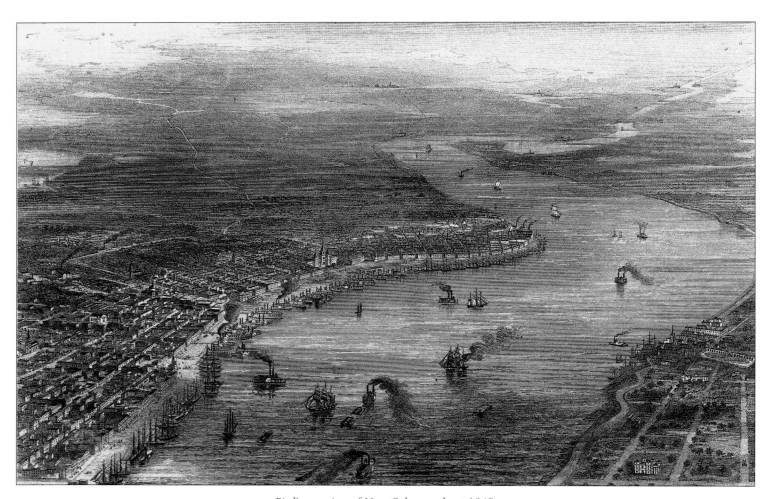

Bird's-eye view of New Orleans, about 1845

RIGHT: *St. Louis levee, daguerreotype by Thomas M. Easterly, 1848*

One of the most tragic events in Latter-day Saint river travel began when the dilapidated side-wheeler *Saluda* steamed away from the St. Louis wharf in 1853. Henry Ballard, one of the *Saluda's* passengers, had set sail on 10 January 1852 from Liverpool on the S.S. *Kennebec,* arriving in New Orleans on 14 March. He then transferred to a riverboat, *Pride of the West,* which he indicates would have been better named *Old Frail Craft.* At St. Louis he took passage on the *Saluda* with some seventy-five to ninety other Saints. As they made their way to Council Bluff, the pioneer staging ground, they encountered ice flows and swift currents caused by the spring runoff on the Missouri River. After lying off the port of Lexington, Missouri, the craft's captain decided to make another effort to move upriver on Friday morning, 9 April. Apparently engineers on board allowed the boilers to get dry and red hot, and when the engines started, the cold water being pumped into the boilers caused them to burst, creating a thundering explosion. Ballard recalls: "I was blown about 2 rods and under a bunk with a man with his brains blown out. . . . I was stunned and made senseless for about half an hour. . . . I lost 2 dogs [which he had brought with him from England]. . . . The Lord raised up kind friends that were strangers to me and gave me money to buy provisions."[1]

A number of Saints, possibly twenty-five, were killed and an equal number injured, along with as many as seventy-five other passengers killed. As Ballard notes, the people of Lexington and the crew of another steamboat that was tied up nearby gave aid and comfort to the survivors of the worst disaster on the Big Muddy.

1838 Baltimore and Ohio locomotive

$\mathcal{B}$eginning in 1837 and during the next two decades, most Latter-day Saints traveled as far west as possible by rail toward Church gathering centers and then by water or land to trailheads usually on the Missouri River, ultimately arriving in Utah.

Caroline Hopkins Clark recorded her travel by steam on the water and across the land in 1866. In Canada she confronted British soldiers looking for members of the Irish Revolutionary Brother-Republic, a group who planned to seize Canada in order to coerce Britain into granting Irish freedom during this period (1866–70). She writes:

[June] 7th—We were taken into Castle Gardens today about 12 o'clock. . . . At ten o'clock we had to walk about two miles to a steamboat. . . . We had to sit in the boat all night, so you can guess how comfortable we were. 8th—At break of day we were hurried out to go to the train. We rode all day. . . . Riding in the train is very tiresome. It is something like a galvanic battery, and much faster than we go in England. 9th—We are still riding by rail. We went through British Canada. We were stopped on the road and searched by soldiers for

firearms. We had to change trains at Montreal. . . . 10th—Still continue on by Rail. . . . 11th—We are still journeying by railway. We had to change cars and drop over a river into the United States. There we got refreshments and started again [our] journey. . . . 12th—It is very tedious, riding by rail so long. . . . 14th—Today's journey is a sad one to us, on account of the death of our own dear baby. . . . We left Chicago and proceeded by train to Quincy. We changed trains, and crossed the river. 15th—We took train and proceeded to St. Joseph, and stayed all day and night there. . . . 16th—Then we took a boat and went up the Missouri River. The water is very dirty with undercurrents. We saw Indians on the bank. 17th—We still keep going up the river. We have to be on top deck. We . . . see the moon and stars shining upon us. 18th—We are still on the river. It remains very hot, and the water keeps very muddy all the way. 19th—Arrived in Wyoming, very early in the morning. The heat is very oppressive. You should see the children; they are blistered with the sun. Little Frank's blisters are very bad. We can see something like sparks of fire. They are small insects [fireflies].[2]

The two-level 822-foot railroad suspension bridge near Niagara Falls was completed in early 1855 and was easily one of the major engineering feats of the decade. In 1868 Hans Jorgenson arrived with a large company of Latter-day Saint pioneers in America. He notes the first few days of travel from the ship to Niagara:

About day break in the 11th of August 1868, we, to our great joy, saw the land for which we so long a time had been longing, having now been on the deadly ship 7 weeks and 3 days [37 died on board]. We all felt to thank God, our deliverer, that he had spared our lives and permitted us to see the land of which we had so great hopes and anticipations. We were quarantined 3 days outside of New York and on the 14th we were permitted to put our feet on American soil. On the 15th, 10 o'clock in the evening, we left New York [by] Rail via Albany & Niagara. The train stopped there and we had a splendid view of the great waterfall, and I walked over the great suspension bridge on the 17th.[3]

Niagara Falls poster, 1876

$\mathcal{S}$ketched on the spot by the painter Rufus Zogbaum, the accompanying scene shows passengers on the hard seats of a Union Pacific emigrant car, known as a "Zulu car." Families and unmarried women were assigned to one car and single men to another. Mary Crandal landed in Boston on 23 May 1856 and recalls:

It was Friday when we landed, but the kind captain allowed the passengers to remain on board till Monday, when we continued our journey to Iowa City. We traveled night and day by rail, buying our victuals at the stations, never undressing for more than a week. We stopped about two hours at the beautiful city of Chicago. . . . We arrived in Iowa about the 1st of June. . . . In coming on the cars I put my head out of the window to see some of the beautiful sights as we passed, and lost my bonnet. Then I was bareheaded; but one of the brethren came to the rescue. He had two hats, and lent me one, so I came to camp with a man's hat on, blushing like a red rose, for I had been told that if I put a gentleman's hat on, he had the right to kiss me.[4]

English convert William Driver notes an event that occurred a decade later, in June 1866:

Wednesday 13th. Luggage Train on Fire. Bros. Bates, Pain, Tracey, Miller and others lost a great portion of their luggage, some lost nearly all they had. . . . Our best Bag of Clothes we have found burnt, company allowed us fifty-five dollars damages. Stayed in a Railway shed. . . . Rain, Thunder and Lightning kept us up most all night. . . .
Saturday 16th. Fine Morning, ribs Tender Through sleeping on the Hard boards of a jolting Car.
Tuesday 19th. This morning at 6 A.M. a terrible accident brought us up suddenly, 1 Carriage 4 Wheels off, 1 Top knocked off, one side and end Broken in, 1 Thrown across the Rail, 1 Thrown completely over on its side;

"Immigrants Traveling West," by Rufus Zogbaum, about 1880

we were obliged to batter in the end to get the people out, 3 Carriages off metal [the tracks], not turned over. It seems miraculous how such a catastrophe could occur and no one be seriously injured, as the cars were all full of passengers. . . . Campt and cooked on the Railway, track cleared and we were started again at 1/2 past 12, a Lady gave me potatoes and Pork, all Persons who saw this disaster say it is a miracle how we escaped with our lives. . . .

Wednesday 20th. Noon still at Chicago, help to shift Luggage from the Cars. Left Chicago about 5 P.M. after waiting 20 Hours for the Cars.[5]

Later William Driver reported that the railroad employees said "it was a d— Mormon miracle."[6]

Ox Wagons to the Promised Land

The wheeled conveyances that transported the Saints to Zion were known as covered wagons or "prairie schooners"—adaptations of the heavy Conestoga wagons of Pennsylvania. These wagons, pulled by slow-moving teams of oxen or mules and assisted frequently by the muscle power of the pioneers, could travel only fifteen to twenty miles each day. The wagons' lack of springs encouraged those who were able to walk to do so. Far more dangerous than American Indians on the trek west were accidents such as falling out of the wagon or being caught in a strong current while fording a river. Just as daunting as any new challenge encountered on the plains were the restless mood swings of the weather. Blistering hot days were frequently followed by biting cold nights, and always there was the wind.

The Latter-day Saint pioneers shared much in common with other people going west—the same roads, campsites, ferries, food, wagons, sicknesses, and trail routines. Individuals were accidentally shot or nearly shot, as was the case of Frederick Gardner in 1851. He broke his wagon tongue crossing a river, and while cutting a pole for a replacement, he "was nearly shot while mistaken for a deer."[1]

However, there were differences which separated the Saints from other westering emigrants: They came because a prophet called them to gather. They believed that the Native American people played a role in the redemptive history of the last days. Their trail was not one way but in reality was a two-way road as emigrants heading west met missionaries and Church leaders on their way east. They planned for people to follow them, making improvements when possible. Even though they were a people of diverse backgrounds, languages, and cultures, there was no difference in their hearts—they came to Zion to see the prophet and the temple in the tops of the mountains.

In the unique view below, Marsena Cannon captures George A. Smith without the hairpiece he generally wore. Elder Smith arrived in the Salt Lake Valley in July 1847. He returned to the Missouri River Valley in October 1847 and remained there until 1849. Upon his arrival back to Utah, he led a company of Saints to Iron County in December 1850. He assisted in establishing settlements at Center Creek and Parowan. Elder Smith is recognized as the father of the southern Utah settlements, chief of which was St. George, named in his honor. He died in Salt Lake City on 1 September 1874.

Mary Fielding Smith, painting by Sutcliffe Maudsley, about 1842

George A. Smith, daguerreotype by Marsena Cannon, about 1853

Mary Fielding Smith, wife of the martyred Patriarch Hyrum Smith, made her way to Utah with her small children, including ten-year-old Joseph Fielding Smith (known today as Joseph F. Smith). Apparently she had been told that she would need help in making the journey and would become a problem for those who traveled with her—to which she protested. Her son recalls:

We moved smoothly until we reached a point about mid-way between the Platte and Sweetwater, when one of our best oxen laid down in the yoke as if poisoned and all supposed he would die. . . . At this Father_____ [the captain of the company] came up and seeing the cause of the disturbance he blustered about as if the world were about at an end. "There," said he, "I told you you would have to be helped and that you would be a burden on the company." But in this he was mistaken.[2]

Proving the captain wrong, Mary Fielding Smith produced a bottle of consecrated olive oil and asked her brother and James Lawson if they would please anoint the ox. The men complied, putting the oil on the head of the beast, laying their hands upon it, and rebuking the destroyer. To the astonishment of everyone but Mary, the ox stood up on its feet, and Mary went marching on.

illiam Clayton's guide was used not only by the Latter-day Saint emigrants but also by others on their way west. Such guides were helpful in identifying good camping grounds where water and feed for animals could be found.

While certainly many people suffered from their arduous trip across the plains, many others enjoyed the experience. Mary Senior, a young emigrant in 1862, summarizes her reaction to the journey in a letter home:

> I never enjoyed better health in my life than while crossing the plains, and up to the present time not the least cause for complaint. We arrived in G. S. L. City on September 23rd, having left Florence on June 23rd, being exactly two months, by the day of the month, in crossing the plains, the quickest trip ever known to have been made with ox-teams. We had a good captain in Captain Homer Duncan, whose train I came in; good teamsters and a good time of it altogether; no accidents of any account; no wagons upset, and the best of times with the cattle. I enjoyed myself very much while traveling, each day bringing its own trails, its pleasures and excitements. The journey to me was a source of much enjoyment and pleasure.[3]

By the time pioneers crossed into present-day Nebraska, prairie grasses were tall enough to provide a feast for hungry oxen, mules, horses, and other domestic animals. As the travelers gazed across what looked like an endless ocean of green, many diarists made special note of the beautiful world they saw. The experience of seeing nature up close for the first time remained with many throughout their lives. Elisha Wilbur was seven when he came to Zion and recalls the "unlimited vastness of the sun flowers in bloom," believing it to be one of the most beautiful sights he had ever seen.[4] Additionally, the heavens also provided marvels of their own. In 1853, James Farmer records that "a comet in the heavens" had been seen for several nights in a row.[5]

THE

LATTER-DAY SAINTS'

EMIGRANTS' GUIDE:

BEING A

TABLE OF DISTANCES,

SHOWING ALL THE

SPRINGS, CREEKS, RIVERS, HILLS, MOUNTAINS,
CAMPING PLACES, AND ALL OTHER NOTABLE PLACES,

FROM COUNCIL BLUFFS,

TO THE

VALLEY OF THE GREAT SALT LAKE.

ALSO, THE

LATITUDES, LONGITUDES AND ALTITUDES
OF THE PROMINENT POINTS ON THE ROUTE.

TOGETHER WITH REMARKS ON THE NATURE OF THE LAND,
TIMBER, GRASS, &c.

THE WHOLE ROUTE HAVING BEEN CAREFULLY MEASURED BY A ROADOMETER, AND THE DISTANCE FROM POINT TO POINT, IN ENGLISH MILES, ACCURATELY SHOWN.

BY W. CLAYTON.

ST. LOUIS:
MO. REPUBLICAN STEAM POWER PRESS—CHAMBERS & KNAPP.
1848.

William Clayton's 1848 emigrants' guide

19

PROMINENT POINTS AND REMARKS.	DIST. miles.	From W Qrs. miles.	From C of G S L. miles.
Cache Cave and head of Echo creek: Altitude, 6,070 feet. - - - . Cave in the bluffs north. Several springs along the road, before you arrive here, and one, a quarter of a mile south from the Cave. Plenty of grass, and a good place to camp.	3¾	£65	66
Cold spring, on the right of the road. - This also is a good place to camp, being plenty of grass	2	967	64
Cold spring, south side the road. - - At the foot of a high hill. Good place to camp. After this, you travel down a narrow ravine, between high mountains, till you arrive at Weber river. Not much difficulty for camping down it.	2¼	969¼	61¾
Deep ravine. - - - - - Steep on both banks. After this, you will cross Echo creek a number of times, but in no place very difficult.	1¼	970½	60½
Red fork of Weber river: Alt. 5,301 feet. There is a good camping place a mile before you arrive here. Also, almost any where on the banks of the river. Plenty of timber. The stream abounds with spotted trout.	16	986½	44½
Weber river ford, 4 rods wide, 2 ft. deep. Good to ford. Plenty of grass and timber on both sides the river.	4	990½	40½
Pratt's Pass, to avoid the Kanyon. - The Kanyon is a few miles below, where the river runs between high mountains of rocks. Some emigrants have passed through, but it is dangerous.	½	991	40
East foot of Long hill. - - - There is a small creek descends down the hollow, up which the road is made. There are several springs near the road.	1	992	39
Bridge (over the creek.) - - - Not a bad place to camp.	2¼	994¼	36¾
Summit of Ridge. - - - - The country west looks rough and mountainous. The descent is not pleasant, being mostly on the side hill.	2½	996¾	34¼
Small creek, left of the road. - - Good place to camp. Plenty of grass, water and willows. The road here turns north a quarter of a mile, then west, and ascends a steep hill.	1¾	998½	32½
Kanyon creek, 1 rod wide, 1 foot deep: Lat. 40° 54′ 7″. - - - - You have to crops thi; creek thirteen times, besides two bad swamps. The road is dangerous to wagons, on account of dense, high bushes, trees, and short turns in the road. Good place to camp. (See Note 9.)	2¾	1001¼	29¾
Leave Kanyon creek. - - - Here you turn to the right, and begin to ascend the highest mount'in you cross in the whole journey. You travel through timber, some on side hills, and cross the creek a number of times.	8	1009¼	21¾
Small spring, left of the road. - - You will probably find water in several places, but it is uncertain where, as it runs but a little way in a place, and then sinks in the ear h.	3	1012¼	18¾
Summit of mountain: Altitude, 7,245 feet. You have now a view of the south part of the Valley of the Great Salt Lake. The descent is steep, lengthy, and tedious, on account of stumps in the road.	1	1013¼	17¾

While emigrant guides helped pioneers in numerous ways, nothing could prepare many of them for the experience of handling oxen. Among the pioneer songs that could be heard along the trail was "Whoa, Haw, Buck and Jerry Boy." Apparently Buck and Jerry were oxen. The command *whoa* meant "stop," *haw* meant "turn left," and *gee* meant "turn right."

> With a merry little jig and a gay little song,
> Whoa, haw, Buck and Jerry Boy.
> We trudge our way the whole day long,
> Whoa, haw, Buck and Jerry Boy.
> And though we're covered all over with dust,
> It's better than staying back home to rust.
> We'll reach Salt Lake someday or bust,
> Whoa, haw, Buck and Jerry Boy.
>
> There's a pretty little girl in the outfit ahead,
> Whoa, haw, Buck and Jerry Boy.
> I wish she was by my side instead,
> Whoa, haw, Buck and Jerry Boy.
> Look at her now with a pout on her lips
> As daintily with her fingertips
> She picks for the fire some buffalo chips,
> Whoa, haw, Buck and Jerry Boy.
>
> Oh, tonight we'll dance by the light of the moon,
> Whoa, haw, Buck and Jerry Boy.
> To the fiddler's best and only tune,
> Whoa, haw, Buck and Jerry Boy.
> Holding her hand and stealing a kiss
> But never a step of the dance we miss,
> Never did know a love like this,
> Whoa, haw, Buck and Jerry Boy.

For many European Saints, the first experiences with oxen were frustrating. Mads Christensen recalls: "The oxen were not trained to pull wagons and knew nothing about 'gee' and 'haw' and less about our Danish talk. We had to tie long ropes to the heads of the leader oxen of each team to prevent them from taking their own course. Occasionally some ox would start to bellow and cause a stampede or panic of fear, and away they would run despite our holding tight to their ropes."[6]

A close examination of this image reveals pioneer wagons in the background. Many pioneer diaries reveal the presence of American Indians along the trail. For the most part, Latter-day Saints noted a friendly contact with these people. In August 1852 the James Chaney Snow company passed Scotts Bluff. Company clerk Henry Robinson writes: "At this place we met a large party of [Sioux] Indians and they came to us in a peaceable manner. . . . We immediately opened our stores and supplied them with [flour, meal, coffee, and sugar]. They appeared well satisfied, . . . wishing us great prosperity, and sang songs of joy."[7]

A Willie handcart company member in 1856 writes cheerfully that the first Indians she met "came to our carts and pushed them into camp for us. . . . They left camp and soon returned with fresh buffalo meat, which they traded for clothing and salt."[8] Danish emigrant Peder Nielsen records:

We have come across quite a few Indians who have been very kind to us. Yesterday, for example, we had a heavy hailstorm, and some of the sisters had gone ahead of the company, and when the storm rose, some Indians were near them and they took their hats made with tarpaulin off and held them over the heads of the sisters. We camped near their camp in the evening; they came over to us and got some bread and flour and port, and were very much satisfied.[9]

Rumors did abound about hostile Indian activity along the trail, as young Brigham Henry Roberts recalls about his experience in 1866:

I and a boy about my own age [nine years old] had become interested in some ripening yellow currants

116

Ute Indian encampment, about 1865

proper place beside the wagon to which he was assigned. The fright was thought of for several days, at least by strict adherence to camp rules about staying with your wagon.[10]

In 1865 Franz Christian Grundvig was an eyewitness to the capture of his young bride, Jessiene, by Indians. She had been ill and was being helped by her husband to catch up to the wagon train. At Cottonwood Hollow on 22 September, three days west of Fort Laramie, a group of Indians stampeded the cattle and in the melee wounded thirteen men and attempted to capture at least two women. Grundvig nearly died from five arrows that pierced his body as he attempted to save his wife. He recalls: "Thinking me dead, the Indians left with my wife."[11] He last saw her as she hung limp and helpless across an Indian pony, "unconscious or dead." James P. Anderson notes, "They also roped one girl, 18, . . . but she managed to free herself from the ropes and escaped."[12] Oxen were killed and wagons abandoned. The company moved forward to Fort Bridger, and for the next three weeks Grundvig rode in a bumpy wagon, feeling the anguish and sorrow for the loss of his wife.

Later, when he went to the Endowment House in Salt Lake City to be sealed to her, the clerk asked if his wife was dead. Grundvig said he did not know and then took a few minutes to tell his sad story. "The clerk went into an adjoining room and spoke to President Daniel H. Wells, who followed him back to the doorway. He looked steadily at Brother Grundvig, who returned his gaze. Then President Wells said slowly, 'Your wife is dead.' "[13]

Sometime emigrants got themselves into trouble when they jokingly offered to trade their spouses to Indians. Priscilla Merriman Evans recalls: "My husband in a joking way told an Indian, who admired me, that he would trade me for a pony. He thought no more about it, but the next day here came the Indian with the pony and it was no joke to him. Never was I so frightened in all my life. . . . There was no place to hide and we did not know what to do. The captain was called and they had some difficulty in settling with the Indian without trouble."[14]

along one of the banks of a stream, and lingered until the train had passed over a distant hill. Before we realized it, we were breaking camp regulations. . . . The caps at last filled, we started to catch the train. . . . Coming to the summit of a swale in which the wagon road passed, we saw to our horror three Indians on horseback. . . . Many a time Captain Chipman had warned us of the possibility [of being captured]. . . . It was, therefore, with magnificent terror that we kept on slowly towards these Indians whose faces remained immobile and solemn, with no indication of friendliness given out at all. I approached my savage knowing not what to do, but as I reached about the head of the horse, I gave one wild yell, the Scotch cap full of currants was dropped, and I made a wild dash to get by—and did—whereupon there was a peal of laughter from the three Indians. . . . The running continued until each of us had found his

Sarah Sophia Moulding was three years old when she came to Zion from her home in Pennsylvania. She writes about a child's experience on the trail:

> I was just past three years of age when we made the trip, and Ida, my sister, was about four and a half. . . . We were so thirsty, and the only time we could stop and get a drink from the canteen . . . was when the other wagons stopped. . . . When we did stop to get a drink, I would always have to wait until my sister had her drink because in England, where my parents were from, the older child was always favored and came first in everything. I can remember how I would dance up and down waiting for her to finish getting her drink, and how thirsty I was. . . . At night they had their times of enjoyments, holding meetings and singing songs of Zion. They even danced once in a while. We girls would get out and play with a little girl in the next wagon, who had a set of dishes made of lead. The red ants were so bad, and Mother often had to strip off our clothes to get rid of them, and how they did bite![15]

Daguerreotype of three unidentified pioneer children, about 1853

The family in the photo on the facing page is identified by some as the Joseph H. Byington family, who were LDS converts, though there is no verifiable evidence to support the claim. Nevertheless, the image captures a moment on a western trail that was shared with many westering pioneers, including the Saints.

Eleven-year-old Rachel Emma Simmons recalls how she drove the wagon because her mother's health was "delicate." She writes: "We never [stopped for] a day in consequence of mother's sickness. The Lord fitted her to bear the journey." Rachel's baby sister, named Mary, was born near Independence Rock. For young Rachel the Platte River Valley was dreary, "nothing but unbroken plains [and] white dusty road."

At the end of the day she and some of the other young women in the group "rushed to the river to bathe." One day she returned to camp after dark. There was her "father with a rope, waiting to receive me. I received a very warm reception."[16]

Canadian convert Margaret Judd Clawson was seventeen years old when she crossed the plains with her family in 1849. She recalls one of the experiences of the journey:

> My brother drove an ox team for a widow and her little girl. The little girl was very sweet and amiable, the mother rather peculiar. He said she would ask more questions in a day than ten men could answer in a week. He was a born joker and could no more help joking

than he could help breathing. He could never tell her anything so absurd or ridiculous but what she believed it. He got so tired of her questions, such as "Riley, I wonder how far we have traveled today?" and "I wonder how far we will travel tomorrow?" "I wonder if we will get to water?" "I wonder if we will see any Indians?" and "I wonder what they will do?" "Will they be friendly or savage?" Her wondering got so monotonous he could hardly stand it. At last he had his revenge when we came in sight of Chimney Rock. . . . At the rate we traveled it could be seen several days before we reached it. [When] she began her speculations about the rock, he told her in

a most confidential way that as soon as we got to it, he was going to push it down, that he was sick and tired of hearing so much about Chimney Rock, that it had stood there long enough anyway. . . . Well, she begged and implored him to let it stand that other emigrants might see it who came after us, but he was obdurate. She then threatened to tell Brigham when she got to the Valley. That was always her last resort. Well, he kept her anxiety at fever heat for two days until we were within about a half a mile of it. He then gave in to her pleadings and said he would let it stand. She was so delighted that she gave him an extra good dinner and supper that day.[17]

Pioneer family resting on the trail

119

*T*he beauty of the natural world could not conceal a silent enemy never far from the trail—the deadly cholera. Overcrowding on the ocean ships, on the river steamboats, and at campsites, coupled with the almost total lack of sanitation, caused the disease to run rampant during the 1850s. Few camps were left unscathed by the worst enemy of those heading west. Rebecca Winters was on the trail in 1852, heading toward Zion with the J. C. Snow company, when she succumbed to this killer near Scotts Bluff. Henry Robinson, company clerk, notes: "[14 August] Sister Winters has been sick for a few days. About noon today she was taken worse and Capt. Winters [captain of ten] thought it desirable to stay a few hours till a change took place for better or [worse]. [16 August] Sister Winter died at 7 o'clock pm yesterday."[18]

Captain Winters sent a note to the company: "Sir, we are again on the move, all well, and shall push on as fast as possible to overtake; yours in haste, Winters."[19] The group caught up with the main body on the following day at Fort Laramie. Before they left Rebecca's grave on the north side of the Great Platte River Road, William Reynolds scratched "Rebecca Winters, age 50 years" on an extra wheel rim while his little daughter Ellis held a candle to give light during the night as he did his job.

For decades the grave was left undisturbed next to the railroad track. In September 1995, however, railroad officials moved Rebecca Winters's grave, feeling that visitors were endangered by the numerous trains that passed there each day.

As the vanguard company made their way toward the Salt Lake Valley, they stopped at Fort Bridger, a trading post for emigrants, trappers, and American Indians in present-day Wyoming. Established by two mountain men, James Bridger and Louis Vasques, the fort was purchased by the Church in 1855.

George Teasdale, a member of the 1861 Johnson wagon company, records the daily ritual of camp life for one group who passed by Bridger on their way to the promised land:

Sun rises, camp guard calls up the people, and in a short time all are busy cooking breakfast, washing, dressing children and preparing for the day's journey. Horn blows for prayers, breakfast is dispatched, the voice of the Cap. is heard, "Oh yes, get up the cattle," a general bustle to clear away, pack up and get ready to start. The cattle is corraled, yoked up, hitched up and out we roll once more at half past 8 on our journey to the gathering place of the Saints. Travel 7 miles, corral, water the cattle, get dinner, hitch up and off again over a rough road for 8 miles and corral once more, get supper, and, as it is a fine moon[lit] night, get in groups sitting round the fires talking merrily. Horn blows, we assemble for prayers, and instructions are given relative to our duties by Cap. Johnson, interpreted to the Swiss by Bro. Woodward, the evening hymn and benediction closes the scene and all retire to rest.[20]

During the Civil War, male born citizens of the United States were forced to stop at Fort Bridger and take an oath of allegiance to the country. Noncitizens were forced to take an oath of neutrality.

ABOVE: *"Fort Bridger, Black's Fork of Green River," 1855*

LEFT: *Rebecca Winters's grave marker unveiling, 26 May 1929*

President Heber J. Grant presides at a special ceremony conducted by the Daughters of the American Revolution at one of the few known marked graves on the trail—that of Rebecca Winters. Delia Ina Winters Booth stands on the left of President Grant, with Augusta Winters Grant (Rebecca's granddaughter) and Edith Grant Young on his right. Standing outside of the closed grave site (left) is Mrs. George Mark, Joseph Anderson, Mrs. T. M. Morrow, Mrs. Karp, Mrs. York A. Hinman, Mrs. A. B. Mathers; (right) Dr. Grace R. Hebard, Mrs. Ruth Stannard, Mr. E. M. Westerfel.

From Liverpool to Salt Lake

*I*n 1853 British Mission president Samuel W. Richards and twenty-three-year-old convert Frederick Hawkins Piercy, an accomplished artist and engraver, decided to publish an illustrated travel book to encourage European Latter-day Saints to gather to Zion. Piercy left England for the United States, making sketches of important scenes along the way and writing a detailed narrative of his trip. Upon his return to England in 1854, Piercy handed his research material and sketches to James Linford, an assistant editor for the Church's *Millennial Star,* to prepare for release. With its thirty steel engravings, and bound in red gilt-stamped morocco, *Route from Liverpool to the Great Salt Lake Valley* is considered one of the most beautiful publications in the Church.

Emigrant ship leaving Liverpool, sketch by Frederick Piercy, 1853

In February Frederick Piercy left England for Utah with 313 other Latter-day Saints. As the shore disappeared the English and Welch emigrants sang "Yes, My Native Land, I Love Thee." The company was divided into districts and the married couples were assigned to the middle of the ship, single males forward, and single women aft. Piercy describes the day:

On the 5th day of February 1853, in compliance with previous arrangements, I embarked in the *Jersey* for New Orleans. . . . After looking round the good ship, and tak-ing a peep at the passengers who were to be my companions during the voyage to New Orleans, . . . there was a general muster for examination by the Government Medical Inspector. . . . We were quickly towed down the Mersey, past the Rock Lighthouse and the Fort at the mouth, and the wind being fair, the sails were soon unfurled and filled, and we stood out to sea. Thoughts crowded my brain; of course, I thought of old England. It is impossible to leave the land of one's birth without regret, or to leave one's kindred and friends, even for a few months, without a sigh.[1]

After a forty-four-day voyage in which only one person died, the ship reached the mouth of the Mississippi, where it encountered an anchored ship unable to continue because of the shallow water.

We should have remained there too, had not our crafty old Captain represented his ship as drawing less water than she really did. The consequence was, that in two or three hours a huge Mississippi steam-boat came along side, and having bound herself to us, very soon carried us safely inside the bar. Then another boat of similar appearance took hold of us, and we began to ascend the far-famed and mighty Mississippi. We entered the river by the south-west channel, and passed the Balize or Pilot Station on the east, about three miles from the bar and the Light-house, of which the accompanying wood cut is a representation, on the west, about four miles inland. . . . We arrive at New Orleans on the 21st of March, having had quite a pleasure trip of a little over six weeks' duration.[2]

At Kanesville Frederick Piercy joined the emigrating company under the presidency of Elders Miller and Cooley.

Lighthouse at the mouth of the Mississippi, illustration by Frederick Piercy, 1853

*F*resh meat was a scarce commodity along the trail. Emigrants were constantly on the lookout for buffalo, deer, elk, and waterfowl. This diet was supplemented by berries, nuts, and roots; and when all else failed, by the old stand-bys—bread, beans, and bacon. Frederick Piercy writes about a hunting expedition near Scotts Bluff:

falo or plains buffalo, which supplied many of their needs. The Saints also enjoyed the fresh meat, which they boiled, dried into jerky, or roasted. Additionally, the Saints used the hides for protection and warmth and the fat for candles.

A mature bull stands six-and-a-half feet at the shoulder and weighs more than 1,980 pounds. The bison is agile and

Frederick Piercy's 1853 illustration of Scotts Bluff

Monday, the 18th. . . . Scott's Bluffs were in view all day. They were certainly the most remarkable sight I had seen since I left England. Viewed from the distance at which I sketched them, the shadows were of an intense blue, while the rock illuminated by the setting sun partook of its gold, making a beautiful harmony of colour. They present a very singular appearance, resembling ruined palaces, castellated towers, temples and monuments. In the foreground of the engraving are seen some emigrants hunting buffalo.[3]

Native Americans hunted bison, commonly called buf-

fast despite its large size, and while it can sometimes be approached closely, at other times it will stampede at the slightest provocation. Wilford Woodruff notes that of "all the sights of Buffalo that our eyes beheld [this] was enough to astonish man. . . . The face of the earth was alive & moving like the waves of the sea."[4] Bison once roamed over most of North America in numbers estimated as high as sixty million. Westering pioneers seemed to prefer killing them for their hides and tongues and for sport. The Latter-day Saints were generally the exception to the rule. Brigham Young denounced the wanton killing of the animals, and most Saints abided by his directions.

$\mathcal{F}$rederick Piercy records his arrival in Salt Lake City:

[August] Tuesday, the 9th.—Commenced our journey this morning by getting our mules "mired" in one of the bad crossings of Kanyon Creek, and after many vain attempts to get them out, we at last succeeded by hitching Elder Bigler's horses to the wagon poles. . . . Just before we turned the corner into the Valley we stopped at the creek, and having bathed and changed our clothing we at last entered as the sun was setting beyond the Great Salt Lake. . . . Day's journey about 30 miles, making a total, according to the best account I could keep, of 7840 from Liverpool.[5]

Great Salt Lake City in 1853, as drawn by Frederick Piercy

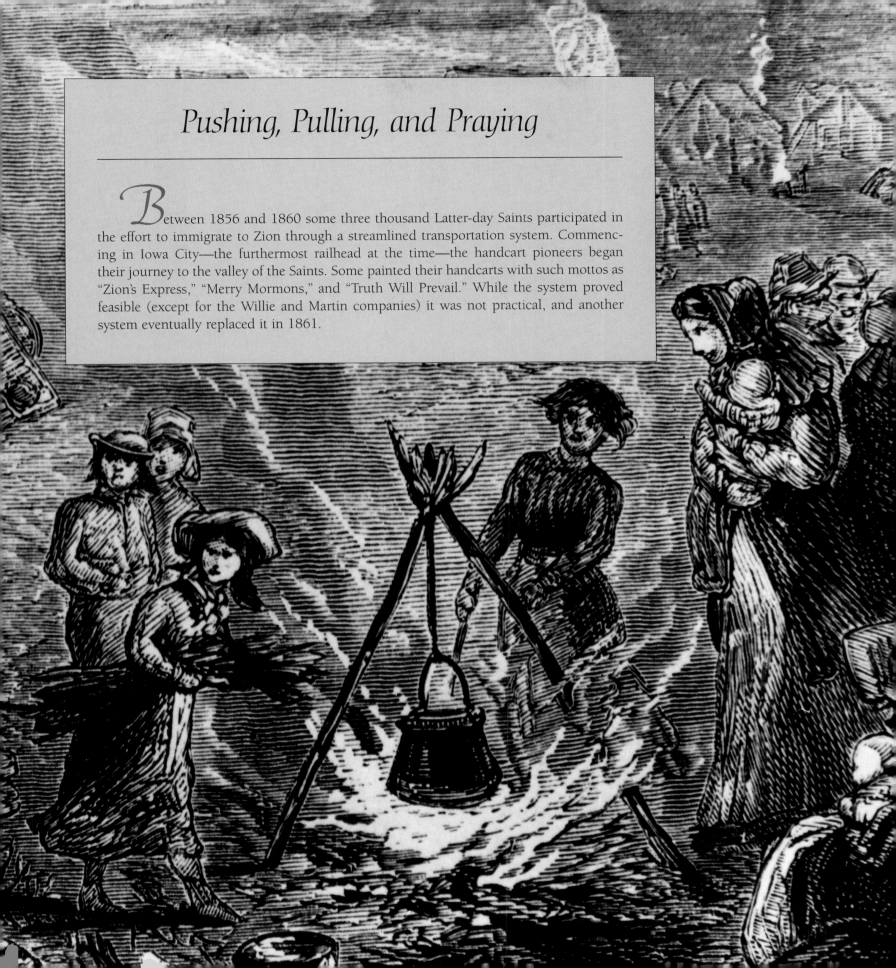

Pushing, Pulling, and Praying

Between 1856 and 1860 some three thousand Latter-day Saints participated in the effort to immigrate to Zion through a streamlined transportation system. Commencing in Iowa City—the furthermost railhead at the time—the handcart pioneers began their journey to the valley of the Saints. Some painted their handcarts with such mottos as "Zion's Express," "Merry Mormons," and "Truth Will Prevail." While the system proved feasible (except for the Willie and Martin companies) it was not practical, and another system eventually replaced it in 1861.

Latter-day Saint elders in Liverpool, 1855

Front row, left to right: James Bond, Spicer Crandall, William C. Dunbar, James Ross, Daniel D. McArthur
Middle row: Edward Bunker, Chauncey Webb, Franklin D. Richards, Daniel Spencer, Dan Jones, Edward Martin
Back row: Edmund Ellsworth, Joseph A. Young, William H. Kimball, George D. Grant, James Ferguson, James A. Little, Philemon Merrill

In 1855, Latter-day Saint elders met in Liverpool to discuss plans to utilize handcarts as a means of bringing Saints to Zion during the 1856 emigration season. Mission president Franklin D. Richards, counselor Daniel Spencer, and Church leaders Dunbar, Bunker, Webb, Martin, Ellsworth, Kimball, Grant, and Ferguson, along with other missionaries as shown in the photo on the facing page, played a significant role in the 1856 emigration from the Missouri River to Salt Lake City.

When these missionaries met in England, the Perpetual Emigrating Fund was severely depleted: As much as $150,000 had been used for the exceptionally heavy emigration of 1855, and the Saints on the Utah frontier were struggling to survive as the clouds of grasshoppers appeared in the valleys of Zion (the famine of 1855–56 was about to descend upon them). To bring more of Europe's poor required a less expensive system than that which was in operation. Church leaders decided to implement the handcart emigration because Church leaders believed "the cry of our poor brethren in foreign lands for deliverance is great, the hand of the oppressor is heavy upon them, and they have no other prospect on earth through which they can hope for assistance."[1]

The handcart trail converged at several key points—Iowa City, New York, Boston, and Liverpool—but in the fall of 1855, one of the trails began in San Germano, in present-day northern Italy. Henriette Chatelain and her brother Pietro left their mountain village with few belongings. Without Church assistance it would have been impossible to make the journey, which they started by walking to Pigneroi from their small village. From this provincial town they made their way to Turin in the center of Piedmont. By train the party went to Susa at the foot of Mount Cenis and then up the steep mountain in a large government coach drawn by sixteen mules. The coach was placed on sleds to make the journey across the Alps to Lanslebourg and then on to Lyons, France. Another train ride to Paris and then on to Calais to board a steamer bound for England. Once they reached Britain's shore, a train took the travelers to Liverpool. At a dock they found the *John Boyd,* a sailing ship.

Charles Savage, a Saint from England who had recently returned from a mission in Switzerland, was notified just days before the ship set sail to accept another assignment: He was to proceed to America, serving as a member of the emigrating company's presidency and, most important, as the interpreter for the group of thirty Italian Saints, many of whom spoke French while on board. He wrote to his fiancée:

> On Board the "John J. Boyd" River Mersey Sunday Night at 19 Dec. 1855
> My dear Annie,
> From the vessell I write to you, some are praying, some are fixing their goods, children crying, some getting in bed and some walking about forming a very curious and interesting sight. . . . I am along with 2 or 3 Scotch families. My company of Italians are not far off. They are not a very bright sample, but they are good, honest hearted souls. . . . I have held two meetings tonight, one in French, and one in English. . . . The President of the ship is Elder [Caunte] Petersen [returning from a four-year mission in his native Norway]. He has the charge of 400 and odd Saints from Denmark [and Norway, Sweden, and Iceland]. I have to look after the [forty-two] English [including Irish and Scottish] and the Italians.[2]

The 1,311-ton American ship sailed from Liverpool on 12 December 1855, arriving in New York after sixty-six days. The Saints were taken to a large hall in Williamsburg. Elder John Taylor arranged for many of the Saints to find employment—shoveling snow, for example—to help support themselves in New York that harsh winter. As spring neared, the Chatelains, along with the other Italian Saints, moved westward to Iowa. Soon others from Europe made their way across the sea to join them at the staging ground near Iowa City, including a group on the *Samuel Curling.*

Mary B. Crandal, a passenger on the *Samuel Curling,* notes their arrival in America: "We landed in Boston May 23rd and remained one day in quarantine. It was Friday when we landed, but the kindhearted captain allowed the passengers to remain on board till Monday, when we continued our journey to Iowa City."[3]

In 1856 the Chicago and Rock Island Railroad reached Iowa City, allowing the Saints to travel by train to the staging ground. Once they passed over the Mississippi River at Rock Island, the train proceeded west through Davenport, Iowa, reaching its terminus at Iowa City. Peter Howard McBride recalls the arrival of his company in 1856: "The night we arrived in Iowa there was the worst storm I ever have experienced, thunder, lightning, rain coming down in torrents. There were wagons to take our bedding and luggage to camp three miles away, but we had to walk. Parents lost their children and children their parents, but we finally got settled in tents for the night, but were all glad when morning came as the sun was shining brightly. It was warm and the people could dry their bedding and clothes."[4]

ABOVE: *Balloon view of Boston in 1860, by James W. Black*

At the Iowa campground, near Iowa City, many interested people arrived in camp to listen to speakers and watch the handcart pioneers get ready for the long, hard march. Among them was Thomas Higgs, an English emigrant who had settled in Davenport a few years before. Apparently his wife had become ill and asked him to find a Latter-day Saint elder to give her a blessing. Her brother, Daniel Stowe, had joined the Church in 1834, followed by her mother, Ann Kite Stowe, in 1841.

John D. T. McAllister, another returning missionary on his way to Salt Lake from England, notes: "Sunday 18th [May]. A.M. very many visitors in Camp. 10 1/2 o'clock, had meeting. Bro. Spencer spoke . . . adjourned for one hour. Half past one, assembled again. Bros. Ellsworth, Bunker, and I addressed the multitude."[5]

This must have been a day of decision for Thomas. Perhaps he had contemplated baptism for some time; perhaps he was touched that day by the spirit of the camp meetings. Regardless, records show that he was baptized in a stream near the camp by Elder Edward Bunker and then confirmed by Elder William Walker. A few days later, another missionary in the group, John Van Cott, records in his journal: "Wednesday 21st—Went to Davenport. . . . In the evening I baptized Elizabeth Higgs, wife of Br. Higgs; returned to the house and confirmed her. During my stay

I was treated very kindly. They rejoiced in the Privilege of having an Elder with them."[6]

Within a few months the Higgs family, including Ann Kite Stowe, were at the campground preparing to head west with the Saints. On 8 August they joined the Hodgett wagon train and moved slowly towards Zion, arriving in December 1856, just behind the Martin handcart company.

Thomas and Elizabeth Higgs family, about 1868
Left to right: Brigham Thomas, Thomas (Zina Maria sitting), Annie Elizabeth (Wallace James standing in front), Elizabeth Stowe (Harriet Eliza lying on lap)

Rufus Wright's painting of Davenport, around 1858

*I*n the year 1856, more than sixteen hundred handcart pioneers left the Latter-day Saint campground near Iowa City. A folk song written by J.D.T. McAllister, "The Handcart Song," became popular in Latter-day Saint communities. It was sung by many British and European Saints who came west across the central plains, pushing and pulling handcarts loaded with food, clothing, bedding, and other personal belongings. The first little group was proud of what it called the Birmingham Band. As they moved westward, the band's playing gave spirit to the people.

*M*any people were interested in these "pushing and pulling" pioneers. A few days after the Willie company left Iowa City, one participant notes, "I would here mention an act of kindness performed by a gentleman (Mr. Charles Good) at Fort Desmoines. He presented me with 15 pairs of children's boots, which I readily accepted as he seemed to be interested by a sincere desire to do good."[7] Others helped along the way: Non-Latter-day Saint farmers and wagon trains shared food, and missionaries and Church leaders heading east often gave what they could, such as a cookie for a child to nibble on during the day.

The first handcart group, which left on 9 June 1856, arrived in Salt Lake City on 26 September. John Bennion notes in his diary the arrival of the handcart pioneers on that particular Sunday: "Went to the city, attended meeting. . . . At noon we went to the Square to view the hand cart company, it being the first that crossed the plains; attended meeting at night at school house."[8]

FACING PAGE: *Ballou's Pictorial, 20 September 1856 issue*

The Handcart Song

Ye saints who dwell on Europe's shore,
Prepare yourselves for many more
To leave behind your native land,
For sure God's judgments are at hand.
For you must cross the raging main
Before the promised land you gain,
And with the faithful make a start
To cross the plains with your handcart.

Chorus
For some must push and some must pull
As we go marching up the hill;
So merrily on the way we go
Until we reach the Valley-o!

As on the roads the carts were pull'd,
'Twould very much surprise the world
To see the old and feeble dame
Thus lend a hand to pull the same!
And maidens fair will dance and sing,
Young men more happy than a king,
And children too will laugh and play;
Their strength increasing day by day.

Chorus

And long before the valley's gained,
We will be met upon the plains
With music sweet and friends so dear
And fresh supplies our hearts to cheer.
And then with music and with song
How cheerfully we'll march along
And thank the day we made a start
To cross the plains with our handcart.

Chorus

M. M. BALLOU, { NUMBER 22 / WINTER STREET.   BOSTON, SATURDAY, SEPTEMBER 20, 1856. $3,00 PER ANNUM. / 6 CENTS SINGLE. { VOL. XI., No. 12.—WHOLE No. 272.

GRANT THORBURN.

The accompanying portrait was drawn for us by Barry, from a painting by Freeman, and is pronounced by competent judges an excellent likeness of the well-known original. Mr. Thorburn was born in Scotland, but has for many years been a citizen of the United States. Galt, the Scotch novelist, introduced him into a romance under the pseudonym of "Laurie Todd," but his actual career, which, in some respects, has been "stranger than fiction," has been delineated in an autobiography, published in New York. Arriving in this country just after attaining his majority, with nothing but his trade (that of a nail-maker) to rely upon, he worked his way up to competence by diligence, industry and resolution. For many years he was a leading seedsman and florist in New York, having had occasion to the adoption of that business. He still pursues this occupation in New Haven, Ct. Though far advanced in life, he is still in the enjoyment of his faculties, as the readers of the "Pictorial" and "Flag of our Union," who have perused his spirited original sketches of the olden time in New York, have had occasion to note. In reply to some inquiries which we addressed him, Mr. Thorburn furnished us with the following memoranda, written in his characteristic style: "I was born in Scotland 18th February, 1773, arrived in New York in my 22d year, a wrought-nail maker by trade. Could only read the Bible and write my own name. In 1802 the cut nails cut me out of employment, and God transformed me into a seedsman—have married three Yankee lasses—one on the 27th of June, 1797, one on the 14th May, 1802, and one on the 12th June, 1853, and the honeymoon is still in the ascendant. Have six children, forty grand-children, and twelve great-grand-Scotch-Yankees. I have been only six days confined by sickness since I saw America; I never was drunk in my life; I never eat enough; I have drank six gills of coffee daily for thirty years past, and smoked six pipes of tobacco every day through the last sixty years (a slow poison in my case). I walk without a staff; I sleep without rocking, and eat my food without the help of brandy or bitters. I wear flannel next my skin summer and winter from my neck to my ankles, hence I never felt a rheumatic pain. The first night I slept on shore was the 17th of June, 1794; the garret was covered with shingles, the

GRANT THORBURN.

roof within five feet of the floor; there was no bed in the garret—I spread my ship mattress on the floor and laid down; the night was *very* hot, and the room alive with fleas, bedbugs and mosquitoes; sleep fled from mine eyes. At midnight the lightning flashed, the thunder roared, and hail and rain drops beat on that shingle roof. I knew not what it meant—we have no shingle roofs in Scotland, no such heavy rain, nor lightning flashing, nor loud thunder. The windows being open the garret seemed on fire—I trembled in every limb. The storm cleared and day broke at three A. M. I rose—head-ache, bone-ache, and spirits sunk down to my heels. I wished myself at *home* again; I had never been twenty miles from the house where I was born till I started for America. Being a stranger, I was loth to disturb the family by going out so early; to improve an hour I opened my small box of books, thinking they wanted airing, having been fourteen weeks in the damp hold of the ship. On the top lay a small pocket Bible; I opened the book. My eye lit on the words, '*My son.*' I thought my father *spoke*: his pious hands placed the book where it might draw my first attention. I read to the end, when, looking up—I had been reading the *third chapter of Proverbs*. The effect was—my headache fled, pain disappeared and my spirits rose ninety-nine per cent. above par; I grasped my nail-hammer and went forth to earn my first sixpence in America, resolving to take this chapter for my *guide* and the sixth verse for my *pilot*. It is sixty-two years since that morning, and often, very often, when not knowing whither to turn, to the right hand or to the left, on turning to this chapter, I found written: '**This is the way—walk ye in it.**'"

MORMONS CROSSING THE PRAIRIE.

The striking scene on this page was drawn for us recently at Fort des Moines, and may be relied on for its fidelity. It was made on the occasion of the transit of a company of Mormons, numbering about six hundred, men, women and children, on their way to Salt Lake, 1400 miles from the fort. They travelled on foot, each family drawing a handcart containing household goods, etc. The train presented a novel sight as it moved on over the great overland route to the Pacific, and though the dwellers on the line see many different kinds of conveyances, the Mormon equipage was something new.

MORMONS CROSSING THE PLAINS.

$\mathcal{E}$nglish convert George Summers made his way to America, leaving his parents and siblings in their native land. Departing on 28 March 1853 aboard the *Falcon,* he finally arrived in Salt Lake City on 16 October 1853. Three years later his sister and brother, having arrived in America, were crossing the plains in two separate companies when word was sent to Church leaders in Salt Lake that the handcart and wagon emigrants were stranded by early winter snow and were facing starvation. The leaders called for a massive rescue effort, and George quickly volunteered to help, along with hundreds of other individuals. His sister Emma recalls her experience with the Willie company: "When they came to the Platte river the saints plunged into the cold freezing water, dragging their carts behind them. That night snow and mud were frozen to their clothes and feet. The next morning many of the saints were found dead or sick. A few days after, a rescue party brought aid."[9]

Apparently George found his sister and, when assured that she was going to survive, sent her on to Salt Lake City. He pressed further east to find his brother Edwin, who was snowbound with the Hunt wagon train.

George Summers, about 1856

$\mathcal{T}$he Martin handcart company and the Hodgett and Hunt wagon companies were found by the express team of Joseph Young, Abel Garr, and Cyrus Wheelock on 28 October, some sixty-five miles east of Devil's Gate. Joseph Young rode back to Devil's Gate to the main rescue party with the news. A log stockade and three or four cabins were located there, and it was decided that the companies had to move as quickly as possible to the site. Men began hauling wood and readying the stockade to house the refugees. As the people staggered into the makeshift relief center, a blizzard struck, leaving twelve to eighteen inches of snow on the ground and a temperature some eleven degrees below zero. After several nights at the stockade, the emigrants were told to cross the Sweetwater River and make camp in a cove about three miles away. Crossing the 90-to-120-feet-wide river, though no more than two feet deep at Devil's Gate, seemed too much for some of the people. Patience Loader could not keep back her tears when she saw the river.[10] Apparently Stephen W. Taylor, David P. Kimball, George W. Grant, and C. Allen Huntington spent most of the

day in the water carrying people across and pulling the handcarts to the other side. When Patience Loader tried to thank David Kimball, he reportedly told her: "Oh, damn that. We don't want any of that. You are welcome."[11]

Writing decades later, Daniel Jones notes his concern about how the story of the rescue was being written: "Some writers have endeavored to make individual heroes of some of our company. I have no remembrance of any one shirking his duty. Each and every one did all they possibly could."[12]

Handcart company in a snowstorm

Devil's Gate on the Sweetwater

*E*nglish convert Jemima Parkes was the first in her family to come to Zion, apparently in 1854. Her mother died in 1854, and during the following year her father and younger sister, Annie, emigrated to America. The father died on the way to the Salt Lake Valley, so young Annie made the remaining part of the journey without family members. Elizabeth, her sister, finally came to America in 1856 and was a member of the Martin handcart company. Her granddaughter writes:

Grandmother would never talk about the trip across the plains. The story of Martin's Handcarts is recorded, and the only knowledge we have of the trip comes from those histories. We have heard from others in the company that on one of the nights when so many had died or were dying, one of the men said to her, "Well, Lizzie, we'll put you in the ground tomorrow." Grandmother rose to the occasion, told him firmly that they would not, and came on. . . . It is typical of her high spirit that she retorted so strongly, and it was perhaps this very remark that made her summon the extra courage to go on. . . . Everyone [from the city] hurried out to meet them [when they arrived in the city]. Jemima went, too. She peeped under the covers of the wagons to see whether or not Elizabeth had come in. . . . Finally she found Elizabeth in one of the wagons. Jemima was so overcome that she went behind a tree until she got control of herself enough to speak. The first thing she said to grandmother was, "Can you walk?" Grandmother, with her usual spirit, replied that she had a great deal of practice and was quite proficient at it. Jemima took her to the Lion House, where Annie was working. All the women there came out to see her, for they had heard that Annie's sister was coming. They took her in, provided her with a bath and clean clothes, and found work for her there.[13]

Elizabeth Hannah and Jemima Parkes, about 1856

Albert Jones, a survivor of the 1856 handcart trip, was so grateful for those who came to help that he vowed that he would help others in a similar way if given the opportunity. That opportunity came in the 1860s, when the Church asked for men to go back east to help bring emigrants to the Valley.

"Handcart Pioneers Coming Through Mountains," painting by C.C.A. Christensen

During the 1859 emigrating season, William Atkins records several rather rash marriages as he traveled with the George Rowley handcart company. While on the Sweetwater, a man from Salt Lake found his lost sweetheart among the company and "there was a ceremony on the spot." At the Big Sandy mail station several unkempt and whiskey-soaked mountaineers offered to marry anyone in the group: "To our surprise two of our young women stepped out and said they would marry them, . . . so two weddings were celebrated that day in mountain style."[14]

Swiss-born Mary Ann Stucki records her family's activities as they made their way to Zion by handcart in 1860 as members of the tenth and last company of handcart pioneers: "Father had bought a cow to take along, so we could have milk on the way. . . . He thought he would make a harness and have her pull the cart. . . . One day a group of Indians came riding up on horses. . . . [They] frightened the cow and sent her chasing off with the cart and children. . . . The cow fell into a deep gully and the cart turned upside down. Although the children were under the trunk and bedding, they were unhurt."[15]

Fellow company member Carl Fjeld writes of the day they arrived in the Valley: "On the 24th of September, 1860, we took up our handcarts for the last time; we pulled them fourteen miles on to the campgrounds in Salt Lake City. Here we set them down, never more to realize how heavy they had been, how hard to pull."[16]

Down and Back in a Covered Wagon

From 1861 to 1868, to help increase the number of Saints coming to Zion, the Church provided a new and inexpensive transportation system known as the "down-and-back" Church trains (*down* from Utah and *back* from the Missouri River). It is a story of community solidarity as wagons, teams, and food supplies were gathered from virtually every ward in Utah for the six-month round trip. A typical Church train company consisted of a captain (usually a seasoned teamster), an assistant captain, at least one teamster per wagon, a captain of the night guard, a commissary chief, a chaplain, a clerk, and several night guards. Reaching Utah during August, September, and October of each year (except in 1865 and 1867, when trains were not sent because of the effects of the Civil War in the East and the Black Hawk War in Utah), the Church trains were an important part of the effort to gather out from every nation those who wanted to come home to Zion.

Missionaries in Echo Canyon, about 1866

*T*hough the men in this photograph have traditionally been identified as a group of proselyting elders in Echo Canyon on their way to their fields of labor, they may actually be members of a Church train on their way east to pick up converts. Because of manpower shortages, even full-time proselyting missionaries were sent with Church train companies on the first leg of the trip to their permanent mission field further east. These elders served as teamsters, night herders, or commissary chiefs for many of the trains heading east to the Missouri River. Returning missionaries fulfilled similar duties for westbound wagon trains. The young men sent on the special "mission" to help with a Church train often found it to be a delightful experience. The young teamsters not only avoided summer farmwork but lived an exciting life on the plains. Additionally, they were able to meet the young single emigrant women before any suitors in Utah had a chance.

*J*ohn Riggs Murdock was one of the thirty-three captains who led Church train companies during what may be the most successful period of emigration in nineteenth-century United States history. The first train, captained by David H. Cannon, set out for Florence, Nebraska, on 23 April 1861 (just days after the news of the attack on Fort Sumter by Confederate forces was received). The company picked up 225 converts and began the return trip on 29 May with fifty-seven wagons heading back west. Captains Ira Eldredge, Joseph Horne, Joseph Murdock, Joseph W. Young, and Heber P. Kimball followed with their companies during the first year. These Church train companies, with two hundred wagons and twenty-two hundred oxen, brought 2,556 emigrants and essential goods west and took 150,000 pounds of flour east. Murdock captained five Church train companies both to and from the Missouri River.

Joseph W. Young, about 1860

*Millard County resident John Riggs Murdock,
photograph by Charles R. Savage*

*J*oseph W. Young moved with the Latter-day Saints to Ohio, Missouri, and Illinois with his family, eventually leaving Nauvoo in 1846. As a member of the Mormon Battalion, he arrived in the Salt Lake Valley in September 1847. He served a mission in England from 1850 to 1853 and in Denmark from 1857 to 1858. He and Feramorz Little made successful journeys transporting goods to and from the Missouri River, demonstrating that it was feasible to make single-season trips to the Missouri River Valley and back to Salt Lake.

While mature men served as captains of the Church trains, with the young men acting as teamsters, other seasoned leaders headed east to coordinate the work of outfitting stations on the Missouri River. Church agents such as Feramorz Little, Nathaniel Jones, Jacob Gates, Thomas Taylor, and Joseph W. Young made the system work. They not only housed and fed the emigrants until they left on the trail toward Zion, but purchased wagons, oxen, and provisions for independent Latter-day Saint emigration companies who came across the trail during the same period.

*N*ew-York-born Orley Dewight Bliss was personally called "to gather the poor" in 1863 and became a down-and-back missionary.[1] Orley records in his diary many details of the trip, including the following: "Wed. 18th May. Traveled 12 miles and camped on Sweetwater 2 miles above the upper crossing. It hailed and blew very hard. . . . Here we had a game of ball this afternoon."[2]

Because the South Platte was flooding, the cattle balked at crossing the river, so Orley took off his clothes and jumped in the river to herd them across: "Bro. A. Stratton and myself had walked about 2 miles without anything on except a coat through a vast lot of wagons, meeting men, women and children" before he could retrieve his pants.[3]

At the new LDS town of "Wyoming," above Nebraska City, the group met up with the emigrants who arrived by riverboat. On the westward journey they held several dances, and the young people were getting acquainted: "[July 9] At camp, sparking [flirting] is extensive this evening. . . . [July 19] The boys and girls are heavy on the spark this evening."[4] The company finally arrived in Salt Lake City on 4 October, and Orley arrived home at Toquerville on 27 October. He left Salt Lake on 2 May 1864 for his second "down-and-back" mission.

*F*or years the Rockies seemed to be a virtually impenetrable barrier to pioneer movement across the continent. Fur trapper Robert Stuart's 1812 journey through the low-lying pass now known as South Pass opened the way for subsequent westering people. It was not uncommon for many Saints camped at South Pass to wake up to a blanket of snow in the morning or to take time to have a snowball fight. Many pioneers found opportunities to divert their attention from the tedious journey through recreational activities, especially the "Utah Boys" who had been called on missions to help bring emigrants safely to Zion during the spring and summer. While they performed invaluable service for the Church on the trail and were appreciated by the emigrants for their handling of the oxen and other difficult duties, the teenage boys had their fun with each other and with the emigrants.

Nineteen-year-old Zebulon Jacobs, a driver in one of the "down-and-back" wagon trains, records some of his experiences on the trail:

> [24 July 1861] We were up at daylight and called out the "National Guard" [the Utah Boys] which fired a volley of musketry, and any kind of guns that were handy. Then

Fording the Platte River, photograph by Charles R. Savage, 1866

Latter-day Saint emigrant company near South Pass, photograph by Charles R. Savage, 1866

the "Martial Band" struck up "Hail Columbia" (the band was composed of tin pails, pans, bake-kettle lids, bells, and various instruments of music); then there was another volley by the Guard; and at sunrise, the firing of cannon (which was about 3 inches in length), and concluded the morning performance with an Indian jig.

[17 August] As we woke up in the morning all hands began laughing at each other, as our faces were besmeared with tar and wagon grease. Some of the [Utah] boys from the other camp had paid us a visit and left their compliments upon our faces.

[24 August] About 10 o'clock P.M. we saw a man running towards us. We hailed him and found that he belonged to Heber C. Kimball's train, which was a short distance ahead of us. The Utah Boys had induced him to catch rabbits in Yankee fashion by building a small fire and lying down by it with an open sack for the rabbits to run into, and then hit them on the head with a club, now and then giving a low whistle; other boys going out to drive the rabbits in. All of a sudden the boys gave a yell. The man thought the Indians were upon him, and off he started at full run. He had run about a mile when we stopped him. The fellow was scared out of his wits. The cause of his scare was this, that he knew everything but Yankee tricks. We took him back to his train which was three-fourths of a mile distant.[5]

Non-Latter-day Saint William Henry Jackson "passed through the Mormon corral" on 10 August 1866 on his way west:

The Mormon corral presents a lively, interesting scene, three hundred men, women and children grouped within the space occupied by the encircled wagons very naturally making it so. A few of the families have small tents that are put up both inside and outside the corral; the rest sleeping either in their wagons or under them. The whole outfit is divided into messes of convenient size, and, as soon as camp is located, the first thing to do is to start the fires; those whose duty it is to provide fuel foraging around in every direction for "chips," sage brush, or any other material available, and soon forty or fifty bright little fires are twinkling inside and outside the corral, with coffee pots, frying pans and bake ovens filling the air with appetizing incense. From a little distance one of these encampments, at night, resembles an illuminated city in miniature, and as one approaches near there is usually the sound of revelry. In every Mormon train there are usually some musicians, for they seem to be very fond of song and dance, and as soon as the camp work is done the younger element gather in groups and "trip the light fantastic toe" with as much vim as if they had not had a twenty mile march that day.[6]

Stereo view of a pioneer camp at the border of Wyoming in 1866, by Charles R. Savage

*The earliest
known photograph
of Fort Laramie, 1858*

Several forts were established on the Laramie River: Fort William (1837) was a fur-trading post, Fort John (1841) was an adobe structure eventually purchased by the U.S. Military, and Fort Laramie (1849) was a fort without a wall, often mentioned in LDS emigrant diaries. In 1862 James McKnight notes: "Sunday, September 7. Camp called at 4:30 a.m. Still cool weather. Move at 8 a.m. The chaplain crossed the Platte, visited Fort Laramie and was courteously treated. . . . He also mailed and obtained letters and bought supplies. Nooned [took a midday break] opposite the Fort. Camped on Platte, six miles above the Fort on the north side."[7]

English convert William Wood made his way to Utah with his fiancée, Elizabeth Gentry, in 1862, encountering many difficulties on the trail. William eventually decided to send her ahead while he stayed behind to earn additional funds. The first night after his sweetheart was on her way, Wood discovered that his troubles were not over yet:

I had occasion to go to my bag for some duds, and in taking out what I expected to be white duck sailor overalls and holding them up and examining them, they turned out to be some sort of ladies' unmentionables trimmed and adorned with lace. The eyes of the crowd caught onto it, and in all the long years that have passed, in meeting any of the old friends and comrades who were there that night, this circumstance would be rehearsed and has been given many a good laugh.[8]

*C*harles Savage, a member of the Chipman wagon train in 1866, took the view below of a pioneer company coming through Echo Canyon in present-day Utah. Brigham Henry Roberts, also a member of the Chipman company, writes:

> Winding of the road through the mountainous country that was now approached had a wonderful fascination to me. . . . Echo Canyon had long been an object of the

journey, made so by the teamsters' weird stories of the echoing qualities of the canyon. Soon it was reached, and as the train wound down the red creek and in, the shooting of cannons and the cracking of whips with Indians' war whoops imitated by the teamsters set the echoes flying over the rugged cliffs that rose, perpendicularly for the most part, on the right hand of the stream.[9]

Emigrants in Echo, photograph by Charles R. Savage, 1866

Echo Canyon, photograph by Charles W. Carter, 1866

*T*his photograph shows a "down-and-back" wagon train making its way through Echo Canyon near present-day Sawmill Canyon. The train is delayed by water that has been backed up onto the trail by beaver dams.

Close-up view of Echo Canyon, photograph by Charles W. Carter, about 1866

*A*pparently this photograph was taken at the same time as the preceding photograph. Note the bogged-down wagon in the left-hand section of the image.

Echo Canyon, photograph by Charles W. Carter, about 1866

amuel and Elizabeth Morgan and their sixteen-year-old daughter, Emma, came to America in 1865 and began the trek west with the William S. S. Willes ox team. Emma died about ten miles east of the Platte Bridge in Wyoming Territory on 21 October. Later, Elizabeth died in Echo Canyon and Samuel buried her at or near present-day Hene-fer, Summit County, Utah. Elizabeth was forty-nine years old when she died in December, just days before reaching her goal of entering the Salt Lake Valley.

Elizabeth's long-held dream of establishing her family in Zion so that they could receive the blessings of the temple was not dashed, however. Two sons; a daughter; and her husband, Samuel; were all in Utah by 1879. On 10 April 1894, within a year of the dedication of the Salt Lake Temple, the surviving children—Joseph, Thomas, and Martha Morgan Burris—gathered in one of the rooms of the temple and were sealed as a family to their parents, with others acting as proxy for deceased family members.

Samuel Morgan in England, about 1860

Elizabeth Beddis Morgan in England, about 1860

Near Coalville in 1866, photograph by Charles R. Savage

his 1866 Charles R. Savage photograph shows a company of pioneers "nooning" near Coalville. The route known as the Golden Pass Road down Parley's Canyon replaced the original route through Emigration Canyon. It turned south up the Weber River instead of north down the river. Brigham Henry Roberts writes:

At the mouth of Echo Canyon, the emigrant road turned southeastward up the Weber, and this brought the [1866 Chipman] wagon train to the first Mormon settlement, Coalville. The settlement was composed chiefly of log houses and dugouts along the hillsides and was decidedly a straggly settlement. . . . The place looked ragged enough, with its irregular scramble of soil-covered cabins and the smoke issuing from its chimneys, but, forlorn as it was, it was a grateful site for the emigrants to see something once more like settled life. The "dugouts" spoken of above consisted of small drifts on a level floor into the hillsides, and these blind trenches were covered over with timber and willows covered with dirt. They made perhaps all in all the most comfortable kind of living quarters for the settlers, and they abounded in other settlements of Utah as well as here on the outskirts—Coalville. They were valued for their warmth. Life and living in Utah, even at this time, was primitive enough and simple.[10]

ome twenty thousand converts came to Zion under the carefully planned and well-orchestrated Church train system. Nearly a third of all Latter-day Saint emigrants who walked along the trail to Utah accompanied the "down-and-back" companies. The development of the telegraph system during the period assisted the successful movement of the Saints during this period of emigration. Companies reported their progress to Salt Lake City on occasion, which allowed Church leaders to determine what help was needed during the last stages of the trip. One captain sent the following telegram in 1868: "South Pass City, Sep. 2. Pres. B. Young— My train of fifty-four wagons and five hundred emigrants passed this point to-day. All well. Plenty of provisions to last us. John Gillespie."[11]

As diarists mention so often, people from the Salt Lake Valley continued to come out to meet and help them. George Summers, who had headed east to help snowbound emigrants in 1856, was again on his way back across the trail in 1866 to meet his mother, Susannah Stockhall Summers, who was traveling with the Chipman company. Converted in 1846 by Elders William Thurgood and Charles R. Jones, she began sending her children to Zion within a few years: George (left England in 1853), Edwin (1855), and Emma (1856). A decade later, after her husband refused to go with her, Susannah Summers left her native land with children Richard and Ann Maria. She was fifty-nine years old when she met her eldest son on the plains. Brigham Henry Roberts, a nine-year-old boy in the same company, recalls his entrance into the city of the Saints with this group of pioneers:

When Captain Chipman's ox team swung around the corner of Third South into Main Street, I found myself at the head of the lead yoke in that team. . . . Here the people had turned out to welcome the plains-worn emigrants and were standing on the street sides to greet them. . . . Along the road, perhaps nearly half way from the mouth of Parley's Canyon to the city, I as I strode on ahead of Captain Chipman's team saw a bright-colored, dainty, charming little girl approaching me in the middle of the street. It was a strange meeting, we two. My hair had grown out somewhat. But three month's journey over the plains and through the mountains without hat or coat or shoes for most of the way had wrought havoc with my appearance. My hair stuck out in all directions; the freckles seemed deeper and more plentiful and the features less attractive than when the journey began. Shirt and trousers barely clung to my sturdy form, and my feet were black and cracked but now covered by the shoes taken from the feet of a dead man at a burnt station. These I was wearing in compliment to my entrance into "Zion." Also my face had been more carefully washed that morning. But try as I would, the shock of hair was unmanageable, and so no wonder the dainty little lady was somewhat timid in approaching me. She had on her arm a basket of luscious fruit, peaches, plums, and grapes. These she extended to me, the "ugly duckling" of a boy from the plains, and asked me if I would have some peaches. . . . I finally turned back as best I could to the wagon where Polly was concealed under the wagon cover because of her being a little ashamed of her appearance. Running behind the wheel ox and climbing up on the tongue of the wagon, I called to my sister, and handed to her the fruit, and then scrambled back to the ground and ran for my place at the head of the train and marched on until the head of Main Street was reached.[12]

The End of an Era

On 10 May 1869, the "wedding of the rails" took place at Promontory Summit, Utah. The whole country celebrated as a transcontinental telegraph reported the blow of a silver sledgehammer driving a golden spike to complete the railroad. In Philadelphia the Liberty Bell was rung; in Chicago a seven-mile procession paraded through the streets; in small towns across the country citizens rang church bells; and in New York and Liverpool, Church agents negotiated prices with transportation companies to send the Saints by steam all the way to Utah.

*W*ind power on the sea and ox power on the land had been the hallmarks of Latter-day Saint emigration. High prices had kept most of the Saints from utilizing the expanding steamship system across the Atlantic, but in 1868 Brigham Young wrote to the European Mission president in England: "To enable our immigration to avail themselves of the healthiest portion or portions of the year for better withstanding the changes of habits, diet and climate, and for other good and sufficient reasons, we wish you to employ none but steamships."[1]

More Latter-day Saints crossed the Atlantic on the liner *Wyoming* than on any other steamship. Over a twenty-year period, some thirty-eight crossings carried more than ten thousand emigrants and missionaries. The fastest trip made by any LDS company was on the steamship *Alaska,* built in 1881 in Scotland. Twenty-three Icelandic converts left Liverpool on 10 July 1886 and arrived in New York on 18 July—a remarkable eight-day passage.

S.S. Wyoming

*W*hile certainly the move to steam shaved off time and greatly increased the comfort and safety of passengers, dangers still lurked in the Atlantic. Nine Latter-day Saint emigrant companies crossed the Atlantic on the steamship *Arizona.* The first company departed from Liverpool on 18 October 1879. After reaching America the ship made headlines when, during the return trip to England, she struck a huge iceberg at full speed fifty miles outside of St. Johns, Newfoundland, telescoping twenty-five feet of the bow. The four LDS missionaries on board, as well as the rest of the passengers, were uninjured and eventually made their way to England to begin their labors. The final emigrating company left the British Isles on 11 May 1889.

S.S. Arizona in 1879

On board an emigrant steamship, around 1880

The last year in which "down-and-back" wagon trains were utilized was 1868. Daniel T. McArthur's mule train, one of several Church trains that year, left Springville on 27 April.[2] As they moved east, the group encountered the coming revolution, as described by Don C. Johnson: "Along Echo Canyon the grader's camps were being established to commence work on the Union Pacific. . . . Beyond Ham's Fork, for miles, the graders were at work."[3] Once at Benton, some of the "Utah Boys" saw for the first time the purpose of all the grading along the way. Johnson recalls: "A number of the boys who had never seen a railroad train went to the terminus, four miles distance, Benton City. Just as they reached the town a freight train was crossing the great trestle bridge, the iron horse puffing and blowing and the brazen bell clanging, as it drew the long train into the depot and stopped. The boys were filled with awe and amazement at the sight of the giant of the iron way."[4]

After reaching its destination in the east, the McArthur company waited for six weeks before being joined by three hundred emigrating Saints in early August. Among the group were William and Elizabeth Hardwick Arbon and their four children. The Arbon family had left England aboard the *Constitution* on 24 June, arriving in New York on 5 August. Traveling on the emerging train system, they made their way to Wyoming. A short trip with the McArthur company ended on 5 September "in good shape."[5]

Apparently the last Church-organized wagon companies, led by Edward T. Mumford and John C. Holman, arrived in Salt Lake City on 24–25 September without fanfare—the end of an era was coming to a close, but no one took particular note of it at the time. An independent company of John Doddle departed from Omaha, Nebraska (apparently lacking funds for train travel to the staging grounds in Wyoming), arriving in Utah on 20 October 1868; and a group of sixty-one emigrants, left in New York by some of the previous companies because of sickness, arrived in Salt Lake City on 24 October in a company led by Fred C. Anderson—making them the last to make the journey by wagon.

During the following year the people of the United States turned their attention to Utah.

There, in mid-May 1869, a group of workers, photographers, LDS church representatives, government agents and officers, and business officials of the Central Pacific and Union Pacific Railroads watched the placing of the last silver-bound laurel tie, the fixing of the last steel rail, and the presentation of the golden spike that would bind the two roads from east and west together. The proceedings were relayed to a listening nation by the telegraph operator at Promontory.

Andrew J. Russell photograph of the driving of the golden spike, Promontory Summit, 10 May 1869

Omaha Telegraph: To Everybody: Keep quiet. When the last spike is driven . . . we will say "done." Don't break the circuit, but watch for the blows of the hammer.

Promontory Telegraph: Almost ready. Hats off. Prayer is being offered.

Chicago Telegraph: We understand. All are ready in the East.

Promontory Telegraph: All ready now. The spike will soon be driven. The signal will be three dots for the commencement of the blows.

W. N. Shilling, the telegraph operator at Promontory, had set wires in advance so that the blows to the iron would signal to the rest of the nation.

Promontory Telegraph: DOT. DOT. DOT. DONE.

A *Deseret News* reporter notes in June 1869:

SAFELY ARRIVED—The first fruits of this year's immigration from Europe reached Ogden last evening at five o'clock. They left Liverpool on the steamship *Minnesota* on the 2nd [of June]. . . . A little more than three weeks has brought them the whole distance of the weary way that once took the best part of the year to travel. This being the first company which has come all the way across the continent from the Atlantic to Utah on the Great Highway, their journey will long be remembered as inaugurating an epoch in our history.[6]

BELOW: *Echo Canyon, painting by an unknown artist, 1870, depicting the transition of an era*

The End of an Era

*B*lack converts Samuel and Amanda Chambers took advantage of the new railroad "highway" and came to Zion from the southern United States, arriving in Salt Lake City in 1869. Samuel gave this testimony in 1873:

> I know we are the people of God, we have been led to these peaceful vallies of the mountains, and we enjoy life and many other blessings. I don't get tired of being with the Latter-day Saints, nor of being one of them. . . . I thank God, for my soul burns with love for the many blessings I enjoy. I've been blest from youth up, although in bondage for 20 years after receiving the gospel, yet I kept the faith. I thank God that I ever gathered with the Saints.[7]

Thomas Higgs, about 1870

Samuel D. and Amanda Chambers, about 1908

*N*ot only did many converts make their way to Utah in 1869–70, but President Brigham Young called some two hundred missionaries east during the 1869–70 winter, utilizing the new railway system that linked Utah with the nation. The Church gained new friends in the East and some pioneers baptized family members and friends.

On 14 February 1870, Elder Thomas Higgs, one of the missionaries called east, wrote President Young:

> Dear Brother and Father, for sutch you have allways been to me. It is with Great pleasure that I address these few lines to you to let you known how and ware I am. . . . [I] arrived in Utica on the eleventh, found my foks all well and glad to see me and I was glad to see them. They received us very kindly. . . . My youngest Bro and Oldist sister I believe will embrace the Gospel. . . . My self and Br Galloway are doing the best we can for the Kingdom of God and it is the Kingdom of God or nothing with your servant and br. in the Gospel of Peace, Ths Higgs[8]

Elder Higgs's mission was successful, and he was able to baptize his sister and bring his brother and family to Utah. He reported on his mission at the Tabernacle on 15 May 1870.

$\mathcal{T}$he first all-steam company to travel to Utah's border in 1869 made the journey from Liverpool to Ogden in twenty-four days. Yet the event that caused real celebration took place on 10 January 1870, when the last rail of the Utah Central Railroad was laid, connecting the Latter-day Saint capital with the rest of the nation. The *Deseret News* reported: "The last spike was driven by President Brigham Young. A large steel mallet was used on the occasion. . . . It was elegantly chased; on the top there was engraved a beehive, surmounted by the inscription 'Holiness to the Lord.'"

Soon the first trains began to arrive in the capital city, with emigrants coming from distant lands to begin new lives in Zion.

Salt Lake City, 10 January 1870

*T*hose who gathered to Zion by wind and ox power joined other recent immigrants in returning to their native lands to proclaim the gospel to friends and family. Once their missions were completed, many of them assisted in bringing others home to Utah. J.C.A. Weibye, who left his native Denmark in 1862 and came to Utah in 1868, returned to Denmark on a mission in 1871, utilizing the power of steam almost the entire distance. In 1873 he returned to America with a group of Scandinavian converts. Sixty-one-year-old Mads and fifty-nine-year-old Ane Marie Hansen left Copenhagen by steamer with Elder Weibye on 29 August 1873. The trip to Utah took one month, a far cry from the 112-day journey their seventeen-year-old daughter made just a few years earlier, in 1868.

Jane Meredith Simons, about 1877

*Y*r Arweinydd I Seion ("The Guide to Zion"), published in 1854 by Dan Jones, provided the Welch Saints with instructions for preparing to gather to Zion. Item three states: "Search for history, names, births, marriages and deaths of your ancestors as far as you can, together with your living relatives. The importance of this will be understood by its future consequences better than we can inform you now."[10] One of the ultimate goals of the gathering of the Saints was participation in the ordinances in Zion's temples for the living and the dead. After arriving in the new gathering place, the Saints sent back thousands of letters to their native lands, and in some cases these pioneers took advantage of the new transportation highway and returned to their former homes themselves to gather information.

Jane Meredith Simons made the trip back to Wales more than twenty years after making the pioneer journey to Zion, leaving her home in Bountiful on 1 November 1877. Apparently set apart as a missionary, she spent time gathering family history material, visiting family members, and attending meetings with the missionaries, where she often sang the songs of Zion. Her visit and work completed, she returned home on the steamship *Nevada* on 25 May 1878.[11]

Mads Hansen and Ane Marie Hansen, parents of 1868 emigrant Karen Marie Hansen, about 1878

Louise Cecile Svenson Speierman, about 1863

*Hans Peter Speierman, while serving in the
Danish Army, about 1863*

*L*ouise Cecile Svenson Speierman; her husband, Hans Peter Speierman; and their two sons, Charles Wilhelm and August Alexander; lived in Copenhagen, Denmark. Many Danish citizens were mobilized into the military in late 1863 as war clouds gathered over the country. The Prussian army eventually invaded the following year, disrupting LDS missionary efforts through 1866. Missionary activity then resumed, and in 1868 Hans was among the 521 Danish converts baptized that year. Following his wife's baptism in 1870, the family prepared to emigrate to Zion, leaving in 1875. Departing from Copenhagen on 25 June, their company made its way to Liverpool. They boarded the *Idaho* and departed on 30 June, arriving in New York on 14 July. Though it was the day of steam, the journey was not without death and struggles, as one Swedish member—seventy-year-old Kirsti Svendsen, who had been in poor health at the time of departure—died along the way.

*P*eter Christian Geertsen, an emigrant arriving with the Speierman family at Castle Garden in 1875, notes:

[4 July] We was taken to dock No. 15 [in] New York, from which place we was taken to Castle Garden, where we arrived about 12 a.m. We could get provisions and everything in this place. . . . Money exchange was also here. . . . Thursday July 15th. At 6 a.m. our luggage was checked and put on a boat, which took several hours hard labour. We left the Garden at 11 a.m. and went to dock 1, from where we was taken to Rail Road Depot in Jersey City. We got good and comfortable cars.[12]

The trip across the continent took seven days, with the group arriving in Utah on 22 July. Even this trip witnessed the death of a fifteen-month-old baby before reaching Ogden.

The End of an Era

Latter-day Saint emigrants at Castle Garden, as shown in Frank Leslie's Illustrated newspaper, 22 January 1878

As They Saw It

*T*he Latter-day Saint artists and photographers who came to Zion enriched the lives of their contemporaries as well as the unborn generations that would follow. As these artists painted scenes of their own experiences, their efforts not only preserved their particular view of the gathering but celebrated the lives of the pioneers who traveled to the promised land in the nineteenth century. Additionally, non-LDS emigrants on the trail left word pictures, sketches, and paintings recalling the Latter-day Saint journey, such as this scene by William Henry Jackson entitled "Emigrants at Kanesville."

George Ottinger joined the Church in 1858 and emigrated across the plains in 1861 with the Milo Andrus company. He left a valuable descriptive diary of the journey and made several important sketches and paintings of pioneer scenes along the way. He was the only Latter-day Saint artist to complete a painting while on the trek west. He recorded the story of this painting in his journal: "Our division went into camp at 7 P.M. Near 'Wolf Creek' we buried this evening, using lanterns to light us, on the north side of the bench on a little bluff almost half a mile from the creek west, John Morse; this was very impressive and would make a fine picture. All over head we had a pale of dark black thunder clouds, while the distant horizon was occasionally lit up with flashes of lightning; travelled 12 miles."[1]

George Martin Ottinger painting of the burial of John Morse at Wolf Creek, Nebraska, in 1861

Chimney Rock, by George Martin Ottinger, painted on 3 August 1861

George Ottinger records his first view of the famous landmark in his journal: "Aug. 2nd—Started at Nine O Clock. Nooned from 12 to 4 P.M. and encamped at 7 P.M. on Platt. Had good day, warm. 'Chimney Rock' in sight all the afternoon, distance 19 miles. August 3rd. Left camp at 7:30. Nooned from 1 to 5 P.M., stopping until one of the Sisters was safely delivered of a fine fat boy. Encamped . . . opposite 'Chimney Rock.' 18 Miles."[2]

Ottinger recalls the events surrounding the creation of his painting of Chimney Rock:

I think it was on the 2nd day of August that we first sighted Chimney Rock. On the 3rd we could see the rock all day long. . . . We camped close to Chimney Rock, it being not more than two or three miles away. . . . I determined to start off in the morning, at daylight, to get a sketch of the Rock. I walked until nearly half past ten o'clock, but the Rock seemed as far off as ever. However, at length I got near enough to the Rock to make a sketch. . . . After painting a sketch of the Rock, I caught up with the train, only after it had gotten into camp that evening. We had marched about seventeen miles that day.[3]

. . . reached "Green River" about sundown but did not get over for two or three hours.

GEORGE OTTINGER, 1861

but did not get over for two or three hours.

The barren landscape in the preceding image gives way to an ideal campsite at the Green River, apparently named because of the green mineral deposits on the banks. The cottonwoods along the river offered much-needed shade from the hot sun. Many camp journals make reference to the three most important aspects of the environment along the trail: the fuel supply, feed for animals, and water for people and animals at the campsite. George Ottinger notes in his journal his arrival at the site:

> Saturday, August 31st—Left camp about 1 P.M. Road awful, dusty; drove the teams nearly all day, reached "Green River" about sundown but did not get over for two or three hours. Got ringing wet crossing with the herd of loose cattle. Went into camp about 9 O Clock. Wood, water & grass plenty. 13 mile. Sunday, September 1st—Layed over all day to rest cattle. This is the most pleasant encampment we have had for a long time. Day splendid. Everybody busy shoeing oxen, greasing wagons & washing clothes.[4]

PRECEDING PAGES: *Painting by George Ottinger, "Mormon Emigration Train at Green River, 1861"*

William Henry Jackson, a non-Latter-day Saint, left Davenport, Iowa, on 19 June 1866, making his way by boat and rail to St. Louis. He proceeded up the Missouri River on a steamboat to Nebraska City. Eventually his trip took him to Salt Lake City, where he arrived on 19 October. During his travels as a "bullwhacker" (one hired to drive oxen), he made sketches of his experiences. Later he used these drawings as bases for his famous watercolors now housed at Scotts Bluff National Monument, Gering, Nebraska.

As Jackson made his way to Nebraska City, he writes:

> [23 June] Decided to sleep on the boat. Scattered around to get our traps and some provisions to last us through to Nebraska City. Smith & I went aboard about 10. . . . On the boat with us are some 2 or 300 Mormon Emigrants bound for Utah under care of one of Brigham Young's Agents. They are a curious study & we find a great deal of amusement in observing them. There appear to be several nationalities represented. Some from the lowest class of society & many others very respectable & genteel appearance. They are the exception however.
>
> [24 June] A good many of the Mormons slept on the hurricane deck & the younger females of the party were recipients of a great deal of attention from some of the men.
>
> [25 June] Occupied most of the day as yesterday in observing the Mormons on the lower deck. . . . Us & [the other bullwhackers] with a few exceptions were very anxious to cultivate the acquaintance of the fairer portion. For myself I had no luck except with a couple of sturdy yeomen from England who were sent for by a son of one to farm to the Weber Valley. Most of them intend to become farmers.[5]

RIGHT: *Lightning storm on the plains, painting by William Henry Jackson*

Though it had a reputation for being "a mile wide and an inch deep," the Platte River proved a daunting challenge. Hidden quicksand, sandbars, and occasional deep water during spring floods made the crossing perilous. However, it did provide something important for the pioneers—water.

Crossing the South Platte, painting by William Henry Jackson

William Henry Jackson's dramatic ink wash shows the power of a western thunderstorm. A lightning bolt has just struck a telegraph pole near an emigrant encampment. Stretching from horizon to horizon, fierce thunderstorms would build and break on an almost daily basis across the open prairie. They usually formed by midday and continued, often accompanied by tremendous displays of lightning, late into the evening. J.C.A. Weibye notes in 1862: "All through the night there were lightning, thunder and rain. We Danes have never seen such kind of weather, for the skies were almost like an ocean [of] fire."[6]

*1862 Norwegian emigrant Danquart Anton Weggeland honored those who gathered to Zion in an 1868 painting entitled
"The Pioneers 1847—Blessings Follow Sacrifice—Crossing the Platte"*

Scandinavian handcart pioneers, painting by Danquart Anton Weggeland, 1908

"Sugar Creek," painting by C.C.A. Christensen, about 1885

C.C.A. Christensen's painting "The Handcart Company" appears so often in Church-related publications that one might give it only a quick glance. However, the painting deserves careful attention to details since Christensen is telling a story he knows by personal experience.

Danish converts Carl Christian Nikolai Dorius, his brother Johan Frederik Ferdinand Dorius, and Carl Christian Anton Christensen, better known as C.C.A. Christensen, were serving as missionaries in Norway when they were formally released and given permission to migrate to Zion. They traveled to Liverpool, where, among the other Scandinavian emigrants preparing for the ocean voyage, were three Norwegian young women whom the missionaries planned to marry once they arrived in Salt Lake City. Upon boarding the *Westmoreland* they were counseled to marry before setting sail—each was married within the hour. C.C.A. Christensen and his new wife, Elise Rosalie Scheel, started their honeymoon on board ship. At the trailhead near Iowa City Christensen notes:

> At the campground we encountered our first trials, in that we had to give up books. . . . We were only allowed to take fifteen pounds in weight for each person who was to travel with the handcarts, and that included our tinware for eating, bedding, and any clothing we did not wish to carry ourselves. . . . Our train consisted of between thirty and forty handcarts. Each of these had an average of five persons. . . . It was usually necessary for small children to ride in the handcart which the father, mother, and older brothers and sisters of the family pulled. . . . The sick and the blind women [in the group] were allowed to ride in one of our freight wagons, for we had three wagons drawn by mules, which carried our tents. . . .
>
> [At one of the river crossings] several of the young girls were ferried across by sitting behind a half-naked Indian on horseback. . . . We baked our bread in kettles.

> . . . Women and children helped gather dried "kokasser" [dried animal dung], as we called them in Danish, since on the great plains along the Platte River there were enough of that kind, from the abundant buffalo herds. . . .
>
> Our costumes would look fine at one of our so-called "Hard Times Balls." Our hats . . . assumed the most grotesque shapes. . . . Ladies' skirts and the men's trousers hung in irregular trimmings. . . . The ladies [were not] particular about whether their skirts could hide their poor footwear, if indeed they were well enough off to own a pair of shoes. . . .
>
> A very old man, who had completely lost his sense of smell, came into camp one day, after the rest of us had things somewhat in order, with a skunk which he counted on cooking for soup. This almost made the rest of us leave. He had killed it with his cane and knew nothing about its peculiar means of defense.[7]

Many of the incidents mentioned in Christensen's narrative are found in the painting, which is a composition of several storytelling scenes: pioneers gathering buffalo chips or cooking with a kettle, small children being pulled by their father and an older sibling, individuals without shoes and in well-worn clothing and hats, horse-riding Indians approaching the company, a freight wagon carrying tents—even a man coming into camp with what could be a dead skunk. Additional elements include a couple hugging (Christensen was honeymooning on the plains), a mother nursing her baby, and a woman removing her shoes and stockings before fording the stream.

OVERLEAF: *"The Handcart Company," painting by C.C.A. Christensen, completed about 1900*

Their Faces Toward Zion

"Immigration of the Saints," painting by C.C.A. Christensen, completed in 1878

C.C.A. Christensen recalls his own welcome to Zion:

One can perhaps form vague ideas of our feeling when we finally stopped [in Salt Lake] and were met by kind brothers and sisters, many of whom brought cakes, milk, and other things that for us were so much needed. It was a Sunday, and with the Danish flag on the lead handcart we marched to our last resting place as far as this journey was concerned. . . . A few days later all these pilgrims had disappeared from their last camping place, having found shelter and hospitality among the Saints in Zion.[8]

Jane Rio Baker notes in 1851: "I ascended the hill before us, and had my first view of the city, which is laid out in squares, or blocks as they call them here. . . . I stood and looked; I can hardly anylise my feelings, but I think my prevailing ones were joy and gratitude for the protecting care over me and mine during our long and perillous journey."[9] John Crook writes: "There was the scene before us that we had long looked for and read and sung about, the City of the Saints. Oh what joy filled each bosom at the sight."[10] A few years later, in 1862, Thomas Memmott notes: "Oh, how my heart leaped for joy at the grand sight, the Zion I had so long wished to see."[11]

Zion's Borders Expand

As soon as the first trains began to arrive in Utah in 1869, expansion of the iron highway throughout Zion began. However, it took decades to reach throughout the Latter-day Saint colonizing region. After their arrival by train to Church headquarters, many immigrants and colonizers still loaded wagons and made a trek to a far-flung settlement. Once they arrived in the new settlements, living conditions were in many cases primitive—these Saints were pioneers as much as any other group.

Established on the pioneer trail leading to the Salt Lake Valley, Coalville was first known as Chalk Creek. By 1859 several families has settled there. Later, when coal was discovered nearby, the name of the community was changed to Coalville. The photograph reveals an early Mormon settlement that was typical of the day. Note the number of log cabins still dominating the townsite.

Coalville, Summit County, Utah, about 1870

A Latter-day Saint family, photographed by Andrew J. Russell in 1869

*I*n the photograph at left of Samuel and Mary Bunting Ashton's log cabin in Kaysville, Mary is standing behind her husband in the doorway. They are surrounded by her mother, her three sisters, and five nieces and nephews. The pioneering nature of life on the Latter-day Saint frontier can be noted in this image of the Ashton's home.

*C*onditions on the western frontier were spartan for many individuals until much later, but this scene could be duplicated well into the late nineteenth century. Yet the Pioneer Day celebrations during this period and in the twentieth century emphasize the faith, courage, and sacrifice of the pioneers who accepted the call from the Lord: "For Zion must increase in beauty, and in holiness; her borders must be enlarged; her stakes must be strengthened; yea, verily I say unto you, Zion must arise and put on her beautiful garments" (D&C 82:14).

The interior of a Latter-day Saint home

Their Faces Toward Zion

$\mathcal{A}$s the Church prepared to celebrate its 50th anniversary in April 1880, local bishops were asked to review a list of those Saints still owing money to the Perpetual Emigrating Fund Company. On preprinted forms they furnished such information as the financial and family status of each debt holder. On the first day of the fiftieth annual conference, held in the Assembly Hall on Temple Square, President John Taylor announced that an important action was about to take place:

> While we are assembled together in the capacity of a Conference, it is proper that our hearts and feelings and affections should be turned to God, that we may reflect upon his kindness, his mercy and salvation extended to us as a people; that we may also reflect upon our weaknesses, our infirmities, our follies and our foibles, and be enabled to lay them aside, feeling that we are the Saints of God. . . . On the fiftieth year, in former times, among the

ancients, they had what was termed a year of jubilee. Slaves were liberated. People who were in debt were forgiven their indebtedness—that is, the poor, the needy and the distressed. And we are reflecting upon some things pertaining to that matter, which will be presented in due form.[1]

A day later President Taylor said to the Saints: "Now, we propose to forgive those who are poor and that are struggling with difficulties in life, who have not been able to meet their engagements in this matter [Perpetual Emigrating Fund

debt]; not half the amount that they are due, but the whole."[2]

The entire congregation voted unanimously to sustain the proposition. Consequently, thousands of individuals were released from their debt to the PEF, the combined total of which amounted to $802,000. Among those released was English convert Rachel Arbon. Since her parents had lacked the necessary funds to join the Saints in Zion, and because PEF resources were limited, they decided to send some of their older children to America to prepare the way for the rest.

Rachel came to the United States with help of the PEF in 1864. According to the PEF ledger, she borrowed $65.70 (recorded 31 December 1864) to help make the journey to the promised land a reality. After arriving in the Valley, Rachel married and moved to Richmond, Cache County, and struggled in the new settlement there. In April 1880 the account book indicates that she had not repaid any of the principle nor any of the interest, which now stood at $105.12, with a total amount due of $170.82.

Within a few months of President Taylor's historic announcement, Rachel gave birth to her seventh child, Frederick, on 20 September 1880, but died on 26 December 1880.[3] The PEF ledger page that contains her account information indicates that on 31 December 1880, the end of the fiscal year, the account was cleared.

Above: *Rachel Arbon, about 1865*

186

Charles W. Carter captured the 1880 pioneer parade in Salt Lake City in this view. On the back side he printed a brief description of the event:

The Pioneer Procession of July 24th, 1880
Illustrated by C. W. Carter

In commemoration of the arrival of the 147 Pioneers in the Valley of Salt Lake, under the leadership of the late Prest. B. Young, on the 24 day of July, 1847, it was decided by the Latter-day Saints to celebrate the occasion by organizing a mammoth procession to demonstrate how Utah has grown in population in the 33 years, having now, according to the census, 143,690 inhabitants; and also in celebration of the year of Jubilee, being 50 years since the organization of the Church.

The procession formed on first South Street, led by the surviving Pioneers, and interspersed with a dozen Brass Bands of the City and adjacent settlements, with a three-mile cortege of glittering splendor, took its line of march to Second West Street; there the entire column countermarched to Seventh East Street, thence west to Third East Street, north to South Temple, and west to the Tabernacle, which was very tastefully decorated for the occasion. 15,000 people here enjoyed themselves for a couple of hours with speeches, music and singing. The procession was one hour and a quarter passing the Kimball Block, from whence [this section was] photographed. The different quorums of the Church, female relief societies, nationalities were well represented. Each trade had superbly fitted up wagons festooned with mottoes, banners and inscriptions. The artisans worked at their trades in these temporary workshops. The drama, press, mines, Mormon Battalion, yacht clubs, and 24 young ladies with their partners, a-la-equestrienne, [were] emblematical of the day, and to contrast the residences of '47 with the palatial residences, stores, and places of worship of 1880, a rough log hut, hauled on a wagon by two yoke of cattle, depicted the change successfully.[4]

The pioneer procession of 24 July 1880, photograph by Charles W. Carter

During the Church's jubilee celebration, Helen Mar Whitney began writing an important series on Latter-day Saint history for the *Woman's Exponent.* "This has been proclaimed as a year of jubilee," she notes in the 15 May 1880 issue. "I truly rejoice that I have had the privilege of being numbered with those who have come up through much tribulation and gained a knowledge for myself that this is the work of God."[5]

She adds later: "There seems to be a great curiosity in the minds of strangers about the 'Mormon women,' and I am willing, nay, anxious, that they should know the true history of the faithful women of Mormondom."[6] Included in her series was the story of her own experiences within the Church. The jubilee celebration stimulated many others, including a number of women, to sit down and write the story of their conversion and gathering to Zion. These recollections enrich our lives and preserve a part of the pioneering past.

In the photograph on the right, Minnie and Ernest Broberg are shown sitting and Robert and Sophia are standing. Their parents, Johan and Eva Catherine Andersson Broberg, lived in Sweden. John Broberg, another son, writes:

> My parents moved to Jönköping, a city that [lies] on the Coast of Vitren, a small lake. My father was a machinist employed in a paper factory. My mother and sisters at home kept busy making paper sacks by hand. These were made from the paper father brought home. The money from these sacks was saved to send us to America. My sister Sophia Olund was the first to emigrate. . . . My sister Minnie Peterson came next. Then Annie, then Ernest. My brother Robert and I were the last of the children to come to America. Our mother came next and father last of all.[7]

It was not uncommon for families to send one individual to Zion at a time until all made their way. Eva Broberg finally left Sweden with a group of Saints bound for England. They departed from Liverpool on the S.S. *Wyoming* on 7 June 1890, arriving in Utah shortly thereafter.[8] Eva's husband, the last member of the family to leave their native land, departed with fifty-eight other Swedish Saints on 16 April 1891 for Hull, England. The company departed from Liverpool on 25 April 1891 on the S.S. *Nevada.*[9] Finally, the family was reunited in Utah to begin a new life in Zion.

LEFT: *Helen Mar Whitney*

RIGHT: *Johan and Eva Broberg children, about 1885, in Sweden*

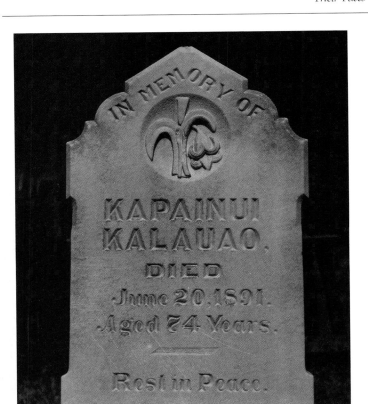

Kapainui Kalauao grave marker, 1891

Fifty years after their arrival to the Great Basin, many of the surviving pioneers of 1847 gathered on Temple Square to have their photograph taken by George Edward Anderson. The oldest surviving pioneer, eighty-nine-year-old Charles Shumway, had been invited to unveil a statue of Brigham Young that would be dedicated on this occasion. Too ill to make the long journey to Salt Lake City from his home in Shumway, Arizona, he nevertheless was thrilled and honored to have been asked. He died within a year, on 21 May 1898.

Not only Europeans flocked to Zion in the nineteenth century. Hawaiian converts came in the 1870s, and by 1889 some seventy-five Saints from the Islands were living in Salt Lake City. Joseph F. Smith, hoping to improve their economic situation, organized the purchase of a ranch west of Tooele in Skull Valley as a gathering place for these poor Saints. The community, established in August 1889, was called *Iosepa,* or "Joseph," after their beloved missionary and friend Joseph F. Smith. Eventually attracting nearly three hundred people, the community was reasonably successful. However, with the construction of the Hawaiian Temple, most residents returned to their native land, and Iosepa was abandoned in 1917. The cemetery, with its Hawaiian names inscribed on memorial stones, is a reminder of the gathering to this spot by faithful Latter-day Saints.

Pioneers of 1847,
photographed by
George Edward Anderson,
24 July 1897

Their Faces Toward Zion

The First Presidency and the Twelve Apostles, 1898
Standing back row, left to right: Anthon H. Lund, John W. Taylor, John Henry Smith, Heber J. Grant, Francis M. Lyman, George Teasdale, Marriner W. Merrill; seated second row, left to right: Brigham Young Jr., George Q. Cannon, Lorenzo Snow, Joseph F. Smith, Franklin D. Richards; seated on the ground, left to right: Matthias F. Cowley and Abraham O. Woodruff

Latter-day Saint colonizers in May 1900, photograph by J. H. Cutler

President Lorenzo Snow called Elder Abraham O. Woodruff to supervise the colonization of the Big Horn Basin in Wyoming. Elder Woodruff asked the "pioneers" to meet at Hams Fork near Kemmerer, Wyoming, on 25 April 1900. More than 250 people from Evanston, Wyoming; Bear Lake and Woodruff, Idaho; and Bountiful, Morgan, and Salt Lake, Utah; gathered at the site, where they were divided into seven companies. The last company left Hams Fork on 3 May 1900. Within three weeks the colonizers gathered near the Shoshone River to officially dedicate the land and their efforts. Elder Woodruff challenged the Saints to work hard and keep the commandments: "I urge you to keep the Word of Wisdom, pay your tithes and offerings. Do not profane the name of Deity. Be honest with all men. Honor the Sabbath day and if you do these things, this will be a land of Zion unto you and your children and children's children throughout the generations that are to come."[10] Within the year the Saints established Basin, Cowley, Kane, and Lovell in the Big Horn Basin.

During the next thirty years Latter-day Saint families established communities in Canada, Samoa, Utah, Idaho, Mexico, New Mexico, and Wyoming. By 1930 the Saints had established more than 740 communities—helping to fulfill the visions of Brother Joseph and Brother Brigham.

*W*hile we generally end the trail story in 1869, with the arrival of the steam train to Utah; and the ocean trek story in 1890, when Church leaders started to counsel Saints to remain in their native lands; the real story continues. Organized LDS emigration companies still brought converts across the ocean to Zion, and Saints continued to pioneer and colonize the North American West through official Church planning well into the twentieth century. Apparently the last officially organized ocean crossing emigrant company set sail on 27 November 1913, when a group of Swedish Saints crossed the ocean on the S.S. *Celtic* from Liverpool. During the first two decades of the twentieth century, several groups of Saints made their way to Zion without the help of the Church emigration office in England.

The Jensen family were part of one such group. Apparently relatives had joined the Church in Denmark and emigrated to Utah sometime earlier. However, a pivotal moment for the family came when a pair of shoes, sent to a cobbler for repair, returned with a missionary tract tucked in one of them. Marius and Maren Jensen were eventually baptized on 9 October 1904 and began to make plans to come to Zion

with their children so that they could enjoy the blessings of the temple. With help from their relatives in Utah, the family made their way to England with several other Scandinavian Saints. The group set sail on 27 March 1906 from a Liverpool dock on the S.S. *Lake Champlain*. They landed at St. Johns, New Brunswick, Canada, on 7 April.[11] After their arrival in Canada, the group made their way by train to the United States border and then proceeded on to Utah. The Jensens came to Hyrum, Cache County, Utah, on 9 April 1906, and on the following day they had their photograph taken to record their arrival in Zion. According to Anna Jensen Jackson:

Our relatives [grandmother Anna Marie Bram Peterson and step-great-grandmother Kristen Marie Hansen] were very angry when they learned we were leaving Denmark. Grandmother Hansen died just a few days after we left. It was a bad trip on the ocean, particularly through the North Sea. Everyone was seasick. The train ride across the continent was long and hard. I was five years old when we came in 1906. Mother and Father wanted to be with the Saints.[12]

Marius and Maren Marie Jensen family, 10 April 1906   Back, left to right: Albert, Marius (seated), Jens (Jim), Maren Marie (seated),
Valdemer (Walter); middle: Anna Marie; front: Viggo (Victor), Elfrida   Front left to right: Viggo (Victor), Elfrieda

Of course, even after 1913 members of the Church found their way to the Latter-day Saint western North American settlements. Following the Second World War, many Saints arrived after fleeing their war-torn countries. More came during the 1950s and 1960s to escape repressive societies in Eastern Europe. At this time Latter-day Saints from the Pacific and Asia made their way to North America to obtain an education or a better job, or just to be with the Saints. Converts from the eastern part of the United States, including black members of the Church, came west, and South and Central Americans and members from Mexico came also. Today, Spanish, Tongan, Samoan, Cambodian, and Vietnamese-language congregations can be found throughout the Latter-day Saint colonization region. Each group and individual enriches the cultural and spiritual aspects of the western North America stakes of Zion.

Epilogue

There is no such thing as a "typical" emigrant story. The pioneers' experiences varied greatly from person to person, company to company, and year to year according to such ever-changing factors as disease and weather. Beneath restless skies, the gathering of the Latter-day Saints brought people together: young and old, rich and poor, educated and uneducated, and those from many different lands. The sacred journey to Zion played a key role in weaving the threads that form the fabric of the Church's history.

𝒫ioneer Day was first celebrated on 24 July 1849, just two years after the vanguard pioneer company entered the Salt Lake Valley. Brigham Young led a small group from his home to the bowery on the Temple Block, where nearly everyone from Salt Lake City had gathered earlier in the day. Following a devotional meeting, the Saints closed the activities of the day with a feast of thanksgiving.

Twenty-three-year-old Albert King Thurber, "bitten by the California gold bug," was on his way west when his group of forty-niners stopped in Salt Lake City just before the first Pioneer Day cele- bration. He notes: "On the 24th of July I joined in the cele- bration and thought that as pretty a scene as I had ever beheld was the 24 young men and women when they came into the Bowery singing 'We are the True Born Sons of Zion.' I was much pleased with the whole proceedings and had found a reli- gious society who believed in nat- ural enjoyment."[1]

Albert joined the Church shortly there- after, letting his fellow adventurers proceed on their jour- ney for gold while he remained with the Saints in Zion.

Since those early years, Latter-day Saints have privately and publicly honored the pioneers through various means: visiting pioneer historical sites; producing works of art cele- brating the journey; writing histories of pioneer men, women, and children; and gathering in groups to watch a parade or participate in a picnic.

Celebrating the past forges a link between people and generations and helps us understand and appreciate that which is common in our lives. When a pioneer describes the sun setting or rising, we know that no matter where we are or when we live, we all see the same sun. When we read a word picture about an emigrant parting from family and friends or a missionary leaving for a field of labor, our hearts are full because there is no difference in the tears shed at parting then and now.

A recent convert from Africa, Russia, India, or any other place can relate to the faith and commitment these pio- neers exhibited as they began new lives in a new land with a new religion. Their choice to follow a prophet to Zion took courage and ded- ication and often sacrifice. In this sense, nothing has really changed.

ABOVE: *Decorative plate based on Currier & Ives "The Rocky Mountains, Emigrants Crossing the Plains," F. F. Palmer, 1866*

This gathering was of the common people purely, of the same class that "heard Jesus gladly" (Mark 12:37), that God must love, because he had "made so many of them."

–B. H. Roberts, immigrant from
England in 1866

Acknowledgments

I wish to thank Cory Maxwell, Jana Erickson, and Rebecca Taylor (Bookcraft); Ronald Reid and Marj Conder (Museum of Church History and Art, Salt Lake City, Utah); William Slaughter, D. Randall Dixon, Ronald Watt, Larry Draper, April Williamsen, and Linda Haslem (Archives Division, Church Historical Department, The Church of Jesus Christ of Latter-day Saints, Salt Lake City, Utah); Veneese Nelson and Melvin Belshore (Church Historical Department, The Church of Jesus Christ of Latter-day Saints, Salt Lake City, Utah); Dorothy Horan (Family History Library, The Church of Jesus Christ of Latter-day Saints, Salt Lake City, Utah); Donald Q. Cannon, Ronald Dennis, and Richard Jensen (Brigham Young University, Provo, Utah); and Wallace Broberg, Carma and Blaine Boudrero, James and Paula Conway, LuAnn Harris, Anna Jensen Jackson, Doug and Karna Jones, Linda Lindsey, Loraine Lowe, R. Q. Shupe, Wayne Sorensen, Maurine Turley, and Cora Wistisen.

I have benefited from the historical research, presentations, and writings of several individuals including Lyndia McDowell Carter, William G. Hartley, John K. Hulmston, Stanley B. Kimball, and Conway B. Sonne.

I express appreciation to my wife, Jeni, who spent numerous hours helping, suggesting, critiquing, and supporting these efforts. Together our hearts turned toward courageous progenitors who came to America to begin new lives, and in particular, toward grandparents born in Europe who confronted another culture, language, and life once they arrived here, giving us and our children opportunities beyond our grandparents' expectations.

Notes

The abbreviations listed below have been used to simplify references in the notes that follow:

FHL   Family History Library, The Church of Jesus Christ of Latter-day Saints, Salt Lake City, Utah

HBLLBYU Harold B. Lee Library, Brigham Young University, Provo, Utah

LDSCA   Archives Division, Church Historical Department, The Church of Jesus Christ of Latter-day Saints, Salt Lake City, Utah

MLUSU   Milton R. Merrill Library, Utah State University, Logan, Utah

MLUU   J. Willard Marriott Library, University of Utah, Salt Lake City, Utah

USHS   Library Archives, Utah State Historical Society, Salt Lake City, Utah

Epigraphs

Joseph Smith, *Teachings of the Prophet Joseph Smith,* sel. Joseph Fielding Smith (Salt Lake City: Deseret Book Co., 1976), p. 37.

Richard Smyth, "Israel, Israel, God Is Calling," *Hymns,* no. 7.

Introduction

1. Marj Conder, "Discussion of Findings," unpublished research paper, in author's possession.
2. Jane Carter Robinson Hindly, "Jane C. Robinson Hindly Reminiscences and Diary," LDSCA.

The Sacred Journey Begins

1. Joseph Knight Jr., "Autobiographical Sketch, 1862," LDSCA.
2. Lucy Mack Smith, *History of Joseph Smith by His Mother,* ed. Preston Nibley (Salt Lake City: Bookcraft, 1954), pp. 195, 196.
3. Emma Smith to Joseph Smith, 9 March 1839, Joseph Smith Papers, LDSCA.
4. Brigham Young Journal, 24 January 1845, LDSCA.
5. *Times and Seasons,* 6 (1 November 1845): 1017.

6. Ibid., pp. 1017–18.
7. Seventies Book B, 29 December 1845, LDSCA.
8. Joseph Smith had prepared the Saints for his departure, and one aspect of that mission had involved giving a small group of Church leaders and their spouses the blessings of the temple, including washings and anointings, the endowment, and sealings. These members could then assist in giving the general body of the Church these ordinances once the temple was completed. See Richard Neitzel Holzapfel and Jeni Broberg Holzapfel, *Women of Nauvoo* (Salt Lake City: Bookcraft, 1992), pp. 119–26.
9. On 28 December 1839 Willard and Jennetta's eldest son, Heber John, died of smallpox at five months of age. Their second son, also named Heber John, is shown in the photo included in this book.
10. Willard Richards Journal, 11 July 1845, LDSCA.
11. *The Odd Fellow,* 31 December 1845, courtesy of Rick Grunder, Syracuse, New York.

Into the Wilderness

1. Patty Bartlett Sessions Diary, LDSCA.
2. Ibid.
3. Mark Twain, *Roughing It* (New York: New American Library, 1972), pp. 96–97.

4. William Clayton Journal, 15 April 1846, LDSCA.

5. William Clayton, "Come, Come, Ye Saints," *Hymns,* no. 30.

6. As quoted in Daniel Tyler, *A Concise History of the Mormon Battalion* (n.p., 1881), pp. 254–55.

7. Journal History of The Church of Jesus Christ of Latter-day Saints, 28 September 1846, LDSCA.

8. Thomas Bullock Journal, 9 October 1846, LDSCA.

9. As quoted in Andrew Jensen, "Manuscript History of Winter Quarters," 8 November 1846, LDSCA.

10. Eliza R. Snow, *The Personal Writings of Eliza Roxcy Snow,* ed. Maureen Ursenbach Beecher (Salt Lake City: University of Utah Press, 1995), pp. 151, 154, 159, 176.

The Camp of Israel

1. Thomas Bullock Journal, April 1847, LDSCA.

2. Wilford Woodruff Journal, 13 April 1847, LDSCA.

3. William Clayton Journal, 24 April 1847, LDSCA.

4. Ibid., 24 May 1847, LDSCA.

5. Wilford Woodruff Journal, 8 July 1847, LDSCA.

6. Ibid.

7. Thomas Bullock Journal, 14 April 1847, LDSCA.

8. William Clayton Journal, 12 July 1847, LDSCA.

9. Wilford Woodruff Journal, 12 July 1847, LDSCA.

10. Ibid., 24 July 1847, LDSCA.

A Holy Nation and a Promised Land

1. Joseph Smith, *Teachings of the Prophet Joseph Smith,* sel. Joseph Fielding Smith (Salt Lake City: Deseret Book Co., 1976), p. 308.

2. Thomas Bullock Minutes, 24 September 1848, LDSCA.

3. Wilford Woodruff Journal, 27 July 1847, LDSCA.

4. Sermon of Brigham Young, delivered in the Old Tabernacle in Salt Lake City, 6 April 1853; in *Journal of Discourses* 1:133.

5. John Grover Diary, 16 August 1852, LDSCA.

To Every Nation and People

1. As quoted in Heber C. Kimball, "Synopsis," *Deseret News,* 14 April 1858.

2. In *History of the Church* 4:375.

3. Addison Pratt, *The Journals of Addison Pratt,* ed. S. George Ellsworth (Salt Lake City: University of Utah Press, 1990), pp. 358–60.

4. As quoted in James R. Clark, comp., *Messages of the First Presidency of The Church of Jesus Christ of Latter-day Saints,* 6 vols. (Salt Lake City: Bookcraft, 1965–75), 1:260.

5. *Deseret News,* 28 April 1875.

6. Johann Peter Johannsen Journal, typescript, courtesy of Cora Wistisen, Bancroft, Idaho.

7. Ibid.

8. Ibid.

9. As quoted in Ronald D. Dennis, *Welsh Mormon Writings* (Provo, Utah: Religious Studies Center, Brigham Young University, 1988), p. 73.

10. Jabez Woodard Journal, 19 August 1853, LDSCA.

11. Ibid.

12. East Indian Mission Index, LDSCA.

13. Ibid.

14. Parley P. Pratt, *Autobiography of Parley P. Pratt* (Salt Lake City: Deseret Book Co., 1994), p. 358.

15. As quoted in William Farrer, Hawaiian Mission Report and Diary, 13 December 1850, HBLLBYU.

16. George Q. Cannon, *My First Mission* (Salt Lake City: Juvenile Instructor Office, 1882), p. 22.

17. Missionary Blessings, 1856, LDSCA.

18. Joseph C. Rich Journal, 1 May 1860, LDSCA.

19. John R. Young, *Memoirs of John R. Young: Utah Pioneer 1847* (Salt Lake City: The Deseret News, 1920), pp. 237–38.

20. John Morgan Journals, 28–29 July 1882, LDSCA.

21. As quoted in Wayne Sorensen oral history interview, 21 May 1996, Los Gatos, California; by author.

22. Lars Christian Johnson to Matilda Johnson, 9 May 1890, courtesy of Cora Wistisen, Bancroft, Idaho.

23. *Latter-day Saints' Millennial Star* 39 (29 September 1890): 618.

24. *Latter-day Saints' Millennial Star* 42 (20 October 1890): 666.

25. As quoted in *Messages of the First Presidency* 2:34, 35.

Across the Ocean

1. As quoted by William Clayton to Brigham Young, 19 August 1840, Brigham Young Papers, LDSCA.

2. Perpetual Emigrating Fund Company, financial accounts 1849–85, LDSCA.

3. British Mission History, 6 April 1852, LDSCA.

4. British Mission, historical records and minutes, 3 September 1852, LDSCA.

5. John Lyon, *Diary of a Voyage from Liverpool to New Orleans* (Salt Lake City, n.p., 1853).

6. Ibid.

7. As cited in William Mulder and A. Russell Mortensen, eds., *Among the Mormons* (New York: Alfred A. Knopf, 1958), pp. 335–36.

8. Norma Hansen Decker, "Utah Pioneers of 1868: The Last Voyage of the Sailing Vessel 'Emerald Isle,'" unpublished manuscript, in author's possession.

9. Hans Jorgenson Journal, 13–20 June 1868, LDSCA.

10. Decker, "Utah Pioneers of 1868."

11. Ibid.

12. Hans Jorgenson Journal, 31 August 1868, LDSCA.

13. Dan Jones to John Davis, 18 April 1849, LDSCA.

14. Jean Rio Griffiths Baker [Pearce] Journal, typescript, HBLLBYU.

15. Jens Christian Anderson Weibye Journal, 20 March 1862, LDSCA.

16. Ibid., 25 March 1862.

17. Ibid., 29 May 1862.

18. Jens Christian Anderson, 29–31 May 1862, LDSCA.

19. Dominique Boudrero's grandson, Charles Wallace Speierman, married Delilah Higgs, the great-granddaughter of Richard and Elizabeth Brazier Hodges.

Steaming on the Water and Across the Land

1. Henry Ballard Journal, typescript, LDSCA.

2. Caroline Hopkins Clark, "Mrs. Clark's Story," *Our Pioneer Heritage* (Salt Lake City: Daughters of Utah Pioneers, 1967), 10:45–47.

3. Hans Jorgenson Journal, 11–17 August 1868, LDSCA.

4. Mary B. Crandal, "Autobiography of a Noble Woman," *Young Woman's Journal* 6 (April 1895): 318.

5. "London to Salt Lake City in 1867: The Diary of William Driver," ed. Frank Driver Reeve, *New Mexico Historical Review* 17 (January 1942): 47–50.

6. Ibid., p. 50.

Ox Wagons to the Promised Land

1. Frederick Gardner, "Autobiography," MLUU.

2. Joseph Fielding Smith, *Life of Joseph F. Smith* (Salt Lake City: Deseret Book Co., 1938), p. 153.

3. Mary Senior to her parents, 6 October 1862, in the *Latter-day Saints' Millennial Star* 24 (8 February 1862): 82.

4. WPA Mormon Diaries Collection, Special Collections, MLUSU.

5. James Farmer Journal, 25 August 1853, USHS.

6. "Mads Fredrick Theobald Christensen," *Our Pioneer Heritage* (Salt Lake City: Daughters of Utah Pioneers, 1966), 9:398.

7. J.C. Snow Company Journal, 13 August 1852, LDSCA.

8. Sarah Ann Ludlum, "Her Journey West," *Treasures of Pioneer Heritage* (Salt Lake City: Daughters of Utah Pioneers, 1952–1957), 5:257.

9. Peder Nielsen Journal, 18 August 1861, USHS.

10. *The Autobiography of B. H. Roberts*, ed. Gary James Bergera (Salt Lake City: Signature Books, 1990), pp. 26–27.

11. Franz Christian Grundvig, *Our Pioneer Heritage* (Salt Lake City: Daughters of Utah Pioneers, 1966), 9:146.

12. James P. Anderson, "Recollections," LDSCA.

13. Preston Nibley, *L.D.S. Stories of Faith and Courage* (Salt Lake City: Bookcraft, 1957), p. 65.

14. "Priscilla Merriman Evans," *Heart Throbs of the West* (Salt Lake City: Daughters of Utah Pioneers, 1948), 9:9.

15. Sarah S. Moulding Gledhill, "Autobiography," MLUSU.

16. Rachel Emma Simons, "Journal," *Heart Throbs of the West* (Salt Lake City: Daughters of Utah Pioneers, 1950), 11:153–63.

17. Margaret Gay Judd Clawson Autobiography, LDSCA.

18. J. C. Snow Company Journal, 13–16 August 1852, LDSCA.

19. Ibid., 16 August 1852.

20. George Teasdale Journal, 16 August 1861, in Journal History of The Church of Jesus Christ of Latter-day Saints, 23 July 1861, LDSCA.

From Liverpool to Salt Lake

1. Frederick Hawkins Piercy, *Route from Liverpool to the Great Salt Lake Valley* (London: Latter-day Saints' Book Depot, 1855), p. 23.

2. Ibid., pp. 28–29.

3. Ibid., p. 91.

4. Wilford Woodruff Journal, 8 May 1847, LDSCA.

5. Piercy, *Route from Liverpool*, pp. 106–7.

Pushing, Pulling, and Praying

1. *Latter-day Saints' Millennial Star* 18 (26 January 1856): 51–52.

2.   Charles R. Savage to Annie Adkins, 19 December 1855, Savage Book of Remembrance, LDSCA.

3.   Mary B. Crandal, "Autobiography of a Noble Woman," *Young Woman's Journal* 6 (April 1895): 318.

4.   Peter Howard McBride, "Items from the Journal of Peter Howard McBride," *Our Pioneer Heritage* (Salt Lake City: Daughters of Utah Pioneers, 1970), 13:360.

5.   John D. T. McAllister Journal, 18 May 1856, HBLLBYU.

6.   John Van Cott Journal, 21 May 1856, HBLLBYU.

7.   Journal History of The Church of Jesus Christ of Latter-day Saints, 9 November 1856, LDSCA.

8.   John Bennion Journal, 26 September 1856, USHS.

9.   "George Summers," unpublished history, courtesy of Dixie Summers Botsford, Ogden, Utah.

10.   Patience Loader Rozsa Archer Autobiography, HBLLBYU.

11.   Ibid.

12.   Daniel W. Jones, *Forty Years Among the Indians* (Salt Lake City: Juvenile Instructor's Office, 1890), p. 68.

13.   "History of Elizabeth Hannah Parkes, Handcart Pioneer of 1856," unpublished manuscript, courtesy of Melvira Barlow, Salt Lake City.

14.   William Atkins, "Recollections," *Heart Throbs of the West* (Salt Lake City: Daughters of Utah Pioneers, 1945), 6:389.

15.   Mary Ann [Stucki] Hafen, *Recollections of a Handcart Pioneer of 1860* (Lincoln: University of Nebraska Press, 1983), pp. 22–23.

16.   Carl Johan Ellefsen Fjeld, "Autobiography," in Andrew Fjeld, *A Brief History of the Fjeld-Fields Family* (Springville, Utah: Art City Publishers, 1946), p. 26.

Down and Back in a Covered Wagon

1.   Orley Dewight Bliss Journal, 2 May 1863, LDSCA.

2.   Ibid., 18 May 1863.

3.   Ibid., 16 June 1863.

4.   Ibid., 9 July 1863; 19 July 1863.

5.   Zebulon Jacobs Journal, in Journal History of The Church of Jesus Christ of Latter-day Saints, 23 September 1861, LDSCA.

6.   *The Diaries of William Henry Jackson,* ed. LeRoy R. Hafen and Ann W. Hafen (Glendale: The Arthur H. Clark Company, 1959), pp. 64–65.

7.   Journal History of The Church of Jesus Christ of Latter-day Saints, 16 October 1862, LDSCA.

8.   William S. Wood Sr. Autobiography, LDSCA.

9.   B.H. Roberts, *The Autobiography of B. H. Roberts,* ed. Gary James Bergera (Salt Lake City: Signature Books, 1990), p. 33.

10.   Ibid., p. 39.

11.   Journal History of The Church of Jesus Christ of Latter-day Saints, 2 September 1868, LDSCA.

12.   Roberts, *Autobiography,* pp. 40–41.

The End of an Era

1.   Brigham Young to Franklin D. Richards, 23 May 1868, Brigham Young Letterbooks, LDSCA.

2.   Don C. Johnson account, in Journal History of The Church of Jesus Christ of Latter-day Saints, 2 September 1868, LDSCA.

3.   Ibid.

4.   Ibid.

5.   Ibid.

6.   Journal History of The Church of Jesus Christ of Latter-day Saints, 25 June 1869, LDSCA.

7.   As quoted in William G. Hartley, "Samuel D. Chambers," *New Era* 4 (June 1974): 48–49.

8.   Thomas Higgs to Brigham Young, 14 February 1870, Brigham Young Papers, LDSCA.

9.   *Deseret News,* 11 January 1870.

10.   Dan Jones, *The Guide to Zion* (Merthyr-Tyfdil, Wales: Dan Jones, 1854), p. 1, courtesy of Ronald D. Dennis, Provo, Utah.

11.   European Emigration Index [ca. 1926], 25 May 1878, LDSCA.

12.   Peter Christian Geertsen Journal, 14–15 July 1875, LDSCA.

As They Saw It

1.   George Martin Ottinger Journal, 25 July 1861, MLUU.

2.   Ibid., 2–3 August 1861.

3.   "Away, Away to the Mountain Dell," *Improvement Era* 10 (July 1907): 645.

4.   George Martin Ottinger Journal, 31 August–1 September 1861.

5.   *The Diaries of William Henry Jackson,* pp. 31–33.

6.   Jens Christian Anderson Weibye Journal, 15 June 1862, LDSCA.

7.   Richard L. Jensen, trans., "By Handcart to Utah: The Account of C.C.A. Christensen," *Nebraska History* 66 (Winter 1985): 337–43.

8.   Ibid., p. 334.

9.   Jane Rio Griffiths Baker [Pearce] Journal, 29 September 1851, HBLLBYU.

10. John Crook Journal, 1856, HBLLBYU.

11. As cited in Stanley B. Kimball, "The Power of Place and the Spirit of Locale: Finding God on Western Trails," *Journal of Mormon History* 16 (1990): 5.

Zion's Borders Expand

1. In Conference Report, April 1880, p. 5.
2. Ibid., p. 62.
3. Perpetual Emigrating Fund Company, financial accounts 1849–85, LDSCA.
4. Charles W. Carter Photographic Collection, LDSCA.
5. *Woman's Exponent,* 15 May 1880.
6. Ibid., 1 July 1880.
7. John C. Broberg, *Early Memories* (n.p., n.d.); courtesy of Wallace Broberg, Murray, Utah.
8. European Emigration Index [ca. 1926], 7 June 1890, LDSCA.

9. Ibid., 25 April 1891.
10. As quoted in Charles A. Welch, *History of the Big Horn Basin* (Salt Lake City: Deseret News Press, 1940). p. 71.
11. "List or Manifest of Alien Passengers for the U.S. Immigration Officer at Port of Arrival," 7 April 1906, FHL.
12. Anna Jensen Jackson oral history interview, 22, 23, 24 May 1996, Greeley, Colorado; by author.

Epilogue

1. Albert King Thurber Journal, 24 July 1847, LDSCA.

Closing Quotation

B.H. Roberts, *The Autobiography of B.H. Roberts,* ed. Gary James Bergera (Salt Lake City: Signature Books, 1990), p. 4.

Sources for Photographs and Illustrations

The abbreviations listed below have been used to simplify the references in the sources that follow:

BYUMA   Museum of Art, Brigham Young University, Provo, Utah

DUP   Pioneer Memorial Museum, National Society Daughters of Utah Pioneers, Salt Lake City, Utah

HBLLBYU   Harold B. Lee Library, Brigham Young University, Provo, Utah

LDSCA   Archives Division, Church Historical Department, The Church of Jesus Christ of Latter-day Saints, Salt Lake City, Utah

MCHA   Museum of Church History and Art, The Church of Jesus Christ of Latter-day Saints, Salt Lake City, Utah

USHS   Utah State Historical Society, Salt Lake City, Utah

Jacket cover

Devil's Slide, Weber River, William Keith, 1874, Sunset Publishing Corporation, Menlow Park, California

Front and back endsheets

Pioneers fording the Platte River, ca. 1866, Philip C. Blair Collection, Manuscripts Division, University of Utah Libraries, Salt Lake City, Utah.

Introduction

Pages 2–3.   "Company 6" of the Big Horn Basin settlers crossing Hams Fork near Kemmerer, Wyoming, J. H. Cutler, 1900, LDSCA.

Page 5.   MCHA.

The Sacred Journey Begins

Pages 6–7.   Squire Murdock home, Norwich, Vermont, George Edward Anderson, 13 October 1911, LDSCA.

Page 8.   MCHA.

Page 9.   MCHA.

Pages 10–11.   Lake County Historical Society, Mentor, Ohio.

Pages 12–13.   New-York Historical Society, New York City, New York.

Page 14.   HBLLBYU.

Page 15.   LDSCA.

Pages 16–17.   BYUMA.

Page 18.   LDSCA.

Page 19.   LDSCA.

Into the Wilderness

Pages 20–21.   "Crossing the Mississippi on the Ice," C.C.A. Christensen, undated, BYUMA.

Steaming on the Water and Across the Land

Pages 102–3.   Cincinnati, Ohio, ca. 1848, Cincinnati Public Library.

Page 104.   Courtesy of James and Paula Conway, Silver Creek, Utah.

Page 105.   Missouri Historical Society, St. Louis, Missouri.

Page 106.   Photo Archives, Smithsonian Institute, Washington, D.C.

Page 107.   New-York Historical Society, New York City, New York.

Pages 108–9.   Library of Congress, Washington, D.C.

Ox Wagons to the Promised Land

Pages 110–11.   Mormon encampment, ca. 1865, USHS.

Page 113.   Left: LDSCA; right: Corbett Collections, MCHA.

Pages 114–15.   LDSCA.

Pages 116–17.   USHS.

Page 118.   LDSCA.

Page 119.   Denver Public Library, Denver, Colorado.

Page 120.   LDSCA.

Page 121.   MCHA.

From Liverpool to Salt Lake

Pages 122–23.   Entrance to Kanesville, Frederick Piercy, 1853, MCHA.

Page 124.   MCHA.

Page 125.   MCHA.

Page 126.   MCHA.

Page 127.   MCHA.

Pushing, Pulling, and Praying

Pages 128–29.   Handcart pioneers, 1874, LDSCA.

Page 130.   LDSCA.

Page 132.   Boston Library, Boston, Massachusetts.

Page 133.   Top: courtesy of Roberta Barker, Salt Lake City, Utah; bottom: Putnam Museum, Davenport, Iowa.

Page 135.   Courtesy of R. Q. Shupe, San Juan Capistrano, California.

Page 136.   Courtesy of Ruth Summers, Kaysville, Utah.

Page 137.   Top: MCHA; bottom: USHS.

Page 138.   Courtesy of Hannah Melvira Barlow, Salt Lake City, Utah.

Page 139.   MCHA.

Down and Back in a Covered Wagon

Pages 140–41.   "Emigrants [at] Needle Rocks," Charles R. Savage, 1867, Nebraska State Historical Society, Lincoln, Nebraska.

Page 142.   LDSCA.

Page 143.   Bottom left: LDSCA; top right: LDSCA.

Page 144.   LDSCA.

Page 145.   LDSCA.

Page 146.   LDSCA.

Page 147.   Library of Congress, Washington, D.C.

Page 148.   Nebraska State Historical Society, Lincoln Nebraska.

Page 149.   LDSCA.

Page 150.   Top: LDSCA; bottom: LDSCA.

Page 151.   Left and right: courtesy of Maurine Turley, Bountiful, Utah.

Page 152.   LDSCA.

The End of an Era

Pages 154–55.   S.S. *Australia,* LDSCA.

Pages 156–57.   Peabody/Essex Museum of Salem, Salem, Massachusetts.

Pages 157.   Bottom: U.S. Naval Historical Center, Washington, D.C.

Pages 158–59.   Library of Congress, Washington, D.C.

Pages 160–61.   Andrew J. Russell Collection, Oakland Museum of California, Oakland, California.

Page 162.   Utah Museum of Fine Art, University of Utah, Salt Lake City, Utah.

Page 163.   Bottom left: LDSCA; top right: courtesy of Roberta Barker, Salt Lake City, Utah.

Page 164.   LDSCA.

Page 165.   Top left: courtesy of Cora Wistisen, Bancroft, Idaho; bottom right: courtesy of Wallace Broberg, Murray, Utah.

Page 166.　Left and right: courtesy of LuAnn Harris, Logan, Utah.

Page 167.　MCHA.

As They Saw It

Pages 168–69.　"Emigrants at Kanesville," William Henry Jackson, undated, Scotts Bluff National Monument, Gering, Nebraska.

Page 170.　MCHA.

Page 171.　MCHA.

Pages 172–73.　MCHA.

Page 175.　Top and bottom: Scotts Bluff National Monument, Gering, Nebraska.

Page 176.　DUP.

Page 177.　MCHA.

Page 178.　MCHA.

Pages 180–81.　MCHA.

Page 181.　Right: MCHA.

Zion's Borders Expand

Pages 182–83.　Pioneer family, USHS.

Page 184.　Bottom: USHS.

Pages 184–85.　Top: Andrew J. Russell Collection, Oakland Museum of California, Oakland, California.

Page 185.　Bottom: USHS.

Page 186.　Courtesy of Cora Wistisen, Bancroft, Idaho.

Page 187.　LDSCA.

Page 188.　LDSCA.

Page 189.　Courtesy of Wallace Broberg, Murray, Utah.

Page 190.　Left: USHS.

Pages 190–91.　LDSCA.

Page 192.　LDSCA.

Page 193.　LDSCA.

Page 194.　Courtesy of Loraine Jackson Lowe, Sheridan, Wyoming.

Pages 196–97.　"This Is the Place" monument, Richard Neitzel Holzapfel, 12 June 1996, Woodland, Utah.

Epilogue

Page 198.　Courtesy of Jeni Broberg Holzapfel, Woodland, Utah.

Index

Italicized page numbers indicate photographs or illustrations.

Index

Index

Index

Index

Moses, on the temple, 48
Moulding, Ida, 118
Moulding, Sarah Sophia, on crossing plains, 118
Mount Cenis, 131
Mount Pisgah, Iowa, 24, *24*
Mountain fever, 41
Mumford, Edward T., 160
Murdock, John Riggs, 61, 143, *143*
Murdock, Joseph, 143
Murray, Carlos, 22
Murray, Mariann, 22
Museum of Church History and Art, 99

Nalimanui, *68*
Nampa, Denmark, 76
Nauvoo, Illinois, 4, 22, 31, 143,
    departure of Saints from, 19
    ferry crossing, 20
Nauvoo Temple, 31, 49
    conference in October 1845, 18
    prayer of dedication, 18
Nebraska, 114
Nebraska City, 144, 174
Needle Rocks, emigrants at, *140–41*
Nephi, 50
Nevada, 50
Nevada (ship), 165, 199
New Bedford, Massachusetts, 55
Newcastle, Australia, 81
New England, 4, 8
New Jerusalem (Jackson County, Missouri), 15
    plat map of, *15*
New Orleans, Louisiana, 80, 82, 83, 96, 104,
    104, 105, 124
New York, 104, 107, 131, 154, 160, 166
New York City, 76, 80, *89–90, 97*
New Zealand mission, 69
Niagara Falls, railroad suspension bridge, 107,
    107
Nielsen, Hans, 60
Nielsen, Peder, on meeting Indians on trail,
    116
Nielson, Jensine, 99
Nielson, John Rudolf, trunk owned by, *99*
Norfolk, 76
North American (ship), 80
North Sea, 194
Norway, 179

Norwich, Vermont, 8
Nuuanu Valley, Hawaii, 68

Oahu, Hawaii, 68
Oakly, Sister, 22
Odd Fellow (Boston weekly), 19
Ogden, Utah, 50, 162, 164, 166
Ohio, 5, 9, 143
Ohio River, 101
Old State Road, 11
Old Tabernacle, sunburst from, 49, *49*
Olund, Sophia Broberg, 188, *189*
Omaha, Nebraska, 160
Only Way to Be Saved (pamphlet), 67, *67*
Ottinger, George Martin, on burial of John
    Morse, 170
    on encampment at Chimney Rock, 171
    paintings: burial of John Morse, *170*; Chim-
        ney Rock, *171*; "Mormon Emigration
        Train at Green River," *172–73*
Ox, of Mary Fielding Smith, anointed, 113

Pacific Islands mission, 55
Pain, Brother, 108
Painesville, Ohio, 11
Palmer, F. F., decorative plate, *198*
Palmyra, New York, 8
Paris, France, 131
Parkes, Annie, 138
Parkes, Elizabeth Hannah, *138*
Parkes, Jemima, 138, *138*
Parley Street, in Nauvoo, 20
Parley's Canyon, 152, 153
Parowan, Utah, 50, 113
Payson, Utah, 50
Pearce, Jane Rio Griffiths Baker. *See* Baker
    [Pearce], Jane Rio Griffiths
Pennsylvania, 118
Pentecostal outpourings, 14
Perpetual Emigrating Fund, 77, 87, 101, 131
    forgiving of debts, 186
    record of, *82,*
Petersen, Caunte, 131
Petersen, Niels, 60
Peterson, Anna Marie Bram, 194
Peterson, Minnie Broberg, 188
Philadelphia, Pennsylvania, 100, *101*, 104, 154
Phillips, William, 94
Photography, and pioneers, 23

Piedmont, Italy, 63, 101, 131
Piercy, Frederick Hawkins, 122, 126
    on arrival in Salt Lake City, 127
    on ocean trip, 124,
    sketches: entrance to Kanesville, *122–23*;
        emigrant ship leaving Liverpool, *124*;
        Salt Lake City, *127*; Scotts Bluff, *126*
Pigneroi, Italy, 131
Pioneer(s), 4
    of 1847, *190–91*
    camp at border of Wyoming, *146*,
    children, *118*
    companies, 36, 37
    family, *119, 182–83*
    food, 126
    Indian trails, 24
    procession of 24 July 1880, 187, *187*
    settlements, 50
    songs, 115
    trail, 4
Pioneer Day, 198
    celebrations, 185
"Pioneers 1847—Blessings Follow Sacrifice—
    Crossing the Platte" (painting), *176*
Pittsburgh, Pennsylvania, 101
Platte Bridge, 151
Platte River, 7, 40, 113, *144*, 147, 175, 179,
    176
Platte Valley, Sand Hills of, *34–35*
Pleasant Grove, Utah, 50
Plymouth, England, dock, *78–79*
Plymouth Brethren, 66
Pond, Benjamin F., 81
Pond, Brother, 24
Prankisto, "Brigham," 67
Pratt, Addison, 55
Pratt, Ann, 55
Pratt, Ellen, 55
Pratt, Frances, 55
Pratt, Lois, 55
Pratt, Orson, 40, 43, 70
    author of tract, 66
Pratt, Parley Parker, 46, 67
    on mission to South America, 67
    preparation for second coming, 5
Pride of the West (riverboat), 105
Promontory Summit, Utah, 154, 160
    driving of golden spike, *160*
Prophecy, 33

Index

Index

Index

Wheelock, Cyrus, 136
White, Samuel, 70
Whitney, Helen Mar, on Latter-day Saint history, 188
   on Winter Quarters, 32
Whitney, Newell K., 18
Whittle, Thomas, 68
"Whoa, Haw, Buck and Jerry Boy" (song), 115
Widerborg, President C., 89
Wilbur, Elisha, on beauty of plains, 114
Willes, William S. S., ox team of, 151
Williamsburg, 131
Willie handcart company, 4, 116, 134
Winchester, Brother, 32
Winter Quarters, 4, 7, 24, 31, 35, 36, 55
   census taken, 26
   laid out, 26
   temporary Church headquarters, 32
Winters, Captain, 120
Winters, Rebecca, 120
   grave marker unveiling, *120*
   grave moved, 120
Wolf Creek, Nebraska, near, *170*
Woman's Exponent, Helen Mar Whitney on Latter-day Saint history, 188
Wood, William, on having luggage switched, 147
Woodard, Jabez, on converts in St. Germain, 63
Woodruff, Abraham O., *192*

on obeying commandments, 193
Woodruff, Idaho, 193
Woodruff, Wilford, *39*
   and Cache Cave, 41
   diary of, 37
   on fishing, 39
   on land of promise, 43
   on seeing buffalo, 126
Woodward, Brother, 121
Wright, Rufus, painting of Davenport, Iowa, *133*
Wyoming, 106
Wyoming, Nebraska, 144
Wyoming (ship), 72, 76, *156-57*, 188

"Yes, My Native Land, I Love Thee" (song), 124
Young, Brigham, *18*, 24, 32, 35, 40, *46*, 126, 153, 198
   "American Moses," 48
   calls missionaries in October 1949 conference, 52
   calls missionaries to East, 163
   colonizing vision of, fulfilled, 193
   enters Valley, 43
   led exodus from Missouri, 18
   on organization of pioneer companies, 37
   on remaining in Nauvoo to complete temple, 18,
   on rescuing Nauvoo poor, 31
   sees vision of Salt Lake Temple, 47

sick, 41
statue of, 190
   on steamship travel, 157
   succeeds Joseph Smith, 18
   and Utah Central Railroad, 164
   worked day and night in Nauvoo Temple, 19
Young, Brigham, Jr., *192*
Young, Clarissa Decker, 36
Young, Edith Grant, *120*
Young, Harriet, 22, 36
Young, Isaac Perry, 36
Young, J., 32
Young, John R., on mission in England, 72
Young, Joseph, 136
Young, Joseph A., *130*
Young, Joseph W., 143, *143*
Young, Lorenzo Zobieski, 36
Yr Arweinydd I Seion ("The Guide to Zion"), 165

ZCMI sign, *48*
Zechariah, on the temple, 48
Zion, 7, 78, 112, 153
   as a gathering place, 50
   new, 35
   as a temple-city, 15
Zogbaum, Rufus, 108
   "Immigrants Traveling West," *108-9*
"Zulu car," 108

221